# ASHBY-DE-LA-ZOUCH

## Seventeenth century life in a small market town

CHRISTOPHER MOXON

© Christopher Moxon 2013. All rights reserved. No part of this book may be used or reproduced without written permission except in the case of brief quotations. Copyright holder may be contacted at moxonchris@aol.com.

Published by Christopher Moxon, printed by Lulu: www.lulu.com

ISBN: 978-1-291-51228-1

The Front Cover shows a detail from a map of the Manor of Ashby-de-la-Zouch, prepared for the Earl of Huntingdon in 1735
*Reproduced by kind permission of the County Records Office for Leicester, Leicestershire and Rutland*

In memory of
H.E.M. (1899-1974)
who was so proud of his home town
and encouraged me to delve into its history

C.M.

# *Contents*

|  |  | *Page* |
|---|---|---:|
| | INTRODUCTION | 9 |
| 1 | GEOGRAPHY & TOPOGRAPHY OF ASHBY | 13 |
| 2 | MEDIAEVAL ASHBY | 21 |
| 3 | DEMOGRAPHY | 30 |
| 4 | TRADE | 35 |
| 5 | SOCIAL STRUCTURE & POOR RELIEF | 52 |
| 6 | AGRICULTURE | 62 |
| 7 | HOUSING | 73 |
| 8 | LAW & ORDER | 81 |
| 9 | EDUCATION | 98 |
| 10 | RELIGION | 118 |
| 11 | THE MANORIAL LORD & THE TOWN COMMUNITY | 139 |
| | NOTES | 154 |
| | INDEX OF NAMES | 167 |

# *Illustrations*

| | |
|---|---|
| Detail of 1735 map of the manor of Ashby | Front Cover |
| Map I – Ashby and neighbourhood | 14 |
| Map II – Town Fields and Parks | 15 |
| Map III – Ashby Town in 1837 | 19 |
| Aerial view – Market Street from the west | 20 |
| Ashby Castle Hastings Tower | 27 |
| St Helen's Church and sundial | 29 |
| Ashby Castle in ruins | 45 |
| Red Lion token of 1669 | 51 |
| Margery Wright Monument | 61 |
| Lamb Inn - with detail of internal timber structure | 74 |
| Bull's Head | 78 |
| Drawing of William Lilly | 102 |
| Drawing of Samuel Shaw | 111 |
| Portrait of Henry Hastings, 3rd Earl of Huntingdon | 119 |
| Portrait of Arthur Hildersham | 124 |
| Butter Cross | 153 |

# *Introduction*

### I. FROM THESIS TO BOOK

IN 1971 I successfully completed a doctoral thesis on *The Social and Economic Development of Ashby-de-la-Zouch from 1570-1720*.

In 1972 Professor Alan Everitt of Leicester University asked me to condense this thesis with a view to the University publishing it as an Occasional Paper. This proposal was strongly supported by my doctoral supervisor, Dr Joan Thirsk. I agreed to do this, but the demands of my career in theatre administration prevented me from completing more than a brief outline.

Forty years later, now retired, I can start on this proposal afresh. Sadly neither Alan Everitt nor Joan Thirsk is still alive, and Leicester University no longer publishes Occasional Papers. But what follows is essentially a condensed version of my thesis. I have augmented this with some more recent research and have omitted much of the technical analysis. I have occasionally changed the emphasis of my earlier conclusions in the light of later research.

One problem that has arisen over the last forty years relates to the references. When I visited California in 1968 to view the Hastings Manuscripts held in the Huntington Library, these manuscripts were largely unsorted and uncatalogued. My references to specific documents therefore indicated the area of the archives where I had found the box in which they were contained. Subsequently this collection has been re-sorted and catalogued. The documents that I saw which have clearly been specified in the new catalogue are therefore given the modern reference. Where there is some doubt I have given my original reference, but have put this in square brackets to indicate that a modern researcher may have to search for this particular document.

## II. WHY DID I SELECT THIS PARTICULAR TOWN AS THE SUBJECT OF MY THESIS?

I was born and spent my childhood in Ashby and this fired my initial interest in its history. But an initial interest in a town's history would not necessarily lead to a work such as this.

My primary reason for undertaking this work is because Ashby-de-la-Zouch is a type of town that has been neglected by historians in the past. There have been several surveys of larger towns; for example, Leicester and Northampton by Professors Hoskins and Everitt. Similarly agricultural communities have been analysed in some detail; for example, in the works of Professor Ault and Dr. Thirsk, and in particular in the study of Wigston Magna by Professor Hoskins. But, with the exception of Professor Everitt's general survey of market towns in *Agrarian History of England and Wales, 1500-1640* (edited by J. Thirsk, 1967), there has been little attempt to analyse the small market town.

Of course Ashby is not a "typical" small market town. For about seventy years – from the last quarter of the sixteenth century until the Civil War– the town had an importance beyond its size because of the national role of its lords, the Earls of Huntingdon. But for many of its inhabitants, their life in this town was probably similar to that of inhabitants of other small market towns.

The numerical and economic importance of small market towns, with their strong links with agriculture, has not been doubted. Professor Everitt has suggested that there were about 760 market towns in England and Wales in the sixteenth century, and of these the great majority were small, serving a limited agricultural neighbourhood, while the large market towns acted both as regional and local centres.[1]

The majority of the population probably visited their local markets more frequently than the larger markets and, as administrative centres, the small towns probably had a greater impact on their inhabitants than the more distant shire towns. In a sense the small market towns acted as capitals of their local areas, and if, as Professor Finberg suggested, after the age of the stagecoaches they *became backwaters, and sank into a death-like trance'* [2] there is the more reason to study these towns in the period immediately before, and at the start of, this decline.

Some of the neglect of small market towns may have stemmed from a lack of evidence. But the volume of evidence concerning Ashby is larger than might be expected from a town whose population during the seventeenth century never exceeded 1,500.

The manorial records for Ashby were carefully preserved by the Hastings family until 1927, when they were bought by Henry E. Huntington and deposited in his library in California. These manorial documents cover a wide range of subjects, although there are many frustrating gaps. The town Rules book survives intact for most of the seventeenth century, although the majority of the court rolls date from after 1660. The collection includes parts of the Churchwardens' accounts and Overseers of the Poor accounts for the first half of the 17th century, and there is a good selection of correspondence between the Earl and his agents concerning the town. In addition the Hastings manuscripts include the family's accounts and rental rolls, petitions from various townspeople, and a large number of land deeds.

Ashby-de-la-Zouch has reasonably complete parish registers from about 1560, with gaps of only a few months during the Civil War. These registers are at the Leicestershire County Record Office, and also in this Office are the inventories for the county, of which, between 1570 and 1720, almost 350 detail the property of Ashby inhabitants. About the same number of wills by Ashby people survive for this period. The County Record Office also contains the school records, including an account book from 1594, miscellaneous parochial records - in particular, documents concerning the administration of certain town charities and the Poor Laws - and, from about 1680, the records of Quarter sessions.

The most important ecclesiastical documents bearing on the religious life of the town are deposited in Leicester City Museum. There is other ecclesiastical material in the Lincoln City Archives, and in Anthony Gilby's correspondence held in Cambridge University Library. Leicester Museum also holds various land deeds and the City records.

Finally, legal documents, the returns from the hearth and poll taxes, and those concerning inns and alehouses have been consulted in the Public Records Office.

III. ACKNOWLEDGEMENTS

I would like to express my grateful thanks to Joan Thirsk and Alan Everitt for their support and encouragement during my initial research; Huntington Library staff both in 1968 and 2013 for their unfailing courtesy and helpfulness and the staff of the County Records Office both at New Walks and, now, Wigston Magna. Ken Hillier and Robert Jones and the staff at Ashby Museum have been very generous in supplying me with material that the Ashby museum has collected during its first thirty years, and Philip Lord has kindly helped me to navigate through the shoals of the internet and to design the layout of this book. But the mistakes, of course, are all mine.

Chris Moxon
August 2013

# ONE

## *Geography & Topography of Ashby*

T HE geographic position of Ashby may be seen in Map I. The town lies about 120 miles from London and lies on the main roads between Leicester and Burton; between Nottingham and Tamworth, and between Derby and Coventry or Oxford.

Its position on these roads is almost its only topographical asset. When John Mackay visited Leicestershire about 1720 he was not impressed. *'Being the most Inland County in England; and consequently, far from any Sea, or any navigable Rivers, you must not suppose it a County of any Trade, nor indeed is it of pleasure'.*[1] Of Ashby, apart from remarking that it was the *'best market for strong Horses in England'*, Mackay noted that *'It affords as good Ale as Burton...and would be as pleasant a Town, were it but as well paved, which may be done; and had it but a River running by it, which can never be done'.*[2]

Mackay wrote, of course, before the Canal Age had transformed inland navigation, yet even the canal that was to bear the name of Ashby-de-la-Zouch did not bring navigation into the town. As Map II shows, the town does stand upon a stream, called the Gilwiskaw. This rises within the parish and later flows into the river Mease, which itself joins the river Trent, some fifteen miles from the source of the Gilwiskaw. Although this stream was strong enough to drive several watermills within the parish, and a number of people have drowned in it, the Gilwiskaw was always too shallow to carry even the lightest traffic. The closest river of any size is the Trent, which, at its nearest point, flows seven miles from Ashby, to the east of Castle Donington. This might have made Ashby important for the distribution of Trent goods to other parts of Leicestershire, had it not been for the steep hills that lie between the town and the river.

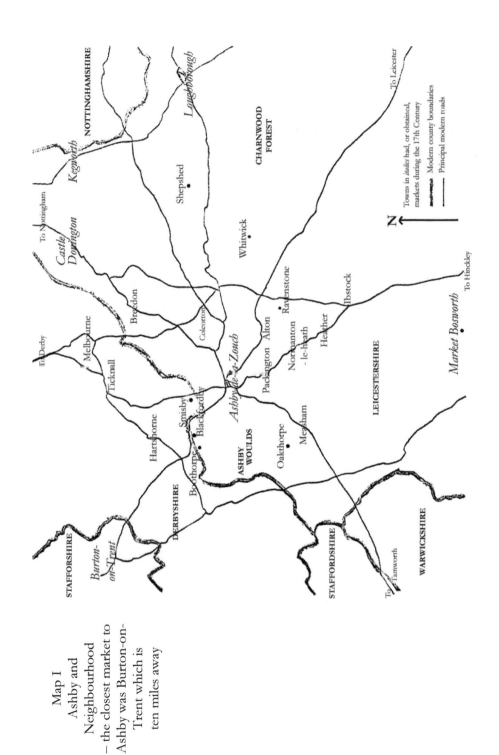

Map I
Ashby and Neighbourhood
– the closest market to Ashby was Burton-on-Trent which is ten miles away

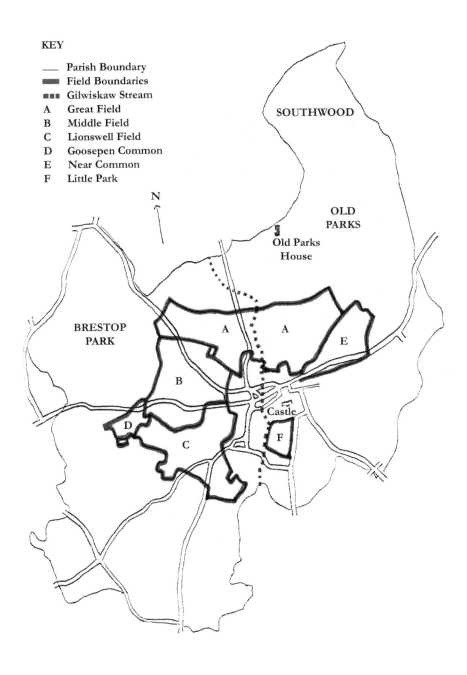

Map II – Ashby: Town Fields & Parks
*(note: roads are shown in their modern position)*

Geologically, Ashby lies some 450 feet above sea-level, at a higher level than its immediate neighbourhood to the south, west and north. Only parts of Charnwood Forest to the east are higher. The parish lies upon a belt of marlstone with Keuper and bunter sandstone, and much of the soil of the area is acid. The area known as Charnwood Forest is still largely barren, although few parts are now wooded; and the names of villages to the south of Ashby - Heather, Donington-le-heath, and Normanton-le-heath - suggest the poorness of the soil in that direction. To the north-east of the town lies an area known as Southwood. The names of the fields into which this was divided – "Thistley pasture", "Stubble close" and no less than five "Rough" closes - suggest that this area could have been of little use as arable land in the seventeenth century. To the west of the town lay an area of about 3,000 acres of waste which was known as Ashby Woulds. A description of this before it was enclosed was made by William Pitt: *'A large area of waste or wet loam, a little but not much encumbered with furze and heath, but for want of drainage, very full of rushes, and sedge grasses.'* [3]

The presence of clay has resulted in the establishment of small potteries about five miles from Ashby, but the principal geological asset of this area has been coal. However coal seems to have played a negligible part in the economy of the town in the seventeenth century. Very little coal lies within the main area of the township, although mines were worked in the seventeenth century on the Woulds and at Coleorton. The Coleorton mines were probably the most important mines in the district and coal had been mined there since the early thirteenth century. These mines, however, were owned by the Beaumont family. The mines on the Woulds were owned by the Hastings but, partly because of the difficulties of transport, these seem to have been run at a loss during much of the seventeenth century. In general, the coal resources of the area were not exploited to any great extent until after the Industrial Revolution.

The layout of the parish may also be seen in Map I. The contiguous villages of Blackfordby and Boothorpe lay to the northwest of Ashby. The distinction between these two villages was not always observed in the seventeenth century. The inhabitants of Boothorpe, which was the smaller of the two villages, were often referred to as inhabitants of Blackfordby and references in this book to Blackfordby may be taken as referring to both these settlements. The ecclesiastical status of Blackfordby chapel within the parish of Ashby was a source of considerable friction during the seventeenth century.

Smisby, to the north of Ashby, was also, at one time, a chapelry within Ashby parish, but seems to have disengaged itself before 1570. Very few of the documents that have been examined referred to inhabitants of Smisby, unless Ashby men were also concerned.

To the southeast of Ashby lay Alton, a deserted village which had been purchased by the Hastings family in the middle of the sixteenth century. 150 years later the ecclesiastical status of this area does not seem to have been settled. In 1696 the farmer of Alton was brought before the Archdeaconry Court concerning his liability to pay church levies to the Ashby churchwardens.

It is also unclear whether or not the Woulds were considered to be within the parish of Ashby. On Map II the parochial boundary is based upon modern parishes, and the areas of the Woulds and of Alton have been excluded.

The manorial boundaries are clearer. The manor certainly included Ashby parish together with Alton and the Woulds. It also included the parishes of Ravenstone and Coleorton.

The township of Ashby-de-la-Zouch formed, then, the centre of a large administrative area, but it is with its central area that this study is primarily concerned.

Ashby absorbed two smaller settlements that had once formed distinct hamlets. The eleventh century village of Ashby was centred on the hill around the castle and church (in modern times, Wood

Street, and Lower and Upper Church Streets).  On another hill half a mile to the west lay the tiny settlement of Kilwardby, a name now applied to the road up this hill.  To the north of Ashby lay a third settlement variously known, in the sixteenth century, as Callis, Netherthorpe or Littlethorpe.  It is possible also that this hamlet may have been known, earlier, as Woodcote (see below, page 62).

Trading seems to have grown up, not in the centre of the original village, but along the road between Ashby and Kilwardby.  The focal point of trading subsequently shifted downhill; away from the original settlement of Ashby, towards the stream that had probably formed the boundary between Ashby and Kilwardby.  As late as 1685 the Earl's steward pointed out that if a particular Ashby man rented the bailiwick *'the markett wilbe againe removed downe towards the bridg and from amongst yor owne tenants.'*[4]  It is significant that the Market Cross, which was demolished in 1827, was sited near the top of Market Street, rather than in the wider area lower down (see illustration, page 153).

One further point may be made about the development of Market Street.  Scarcity of land in towns usually resulted in properties having narrow frontages on the main street with long strips back to a service road.  Ashby's Market Street followed this convention, in so far as it was wider towards the middle of the street and tapered at either end, as can be seen in the aerial photograph overleaf.  Sites with a narrow frontage on Market Street stretched back to two back lanes, but usually only the front part of the site was built upon and the rest of the ground in the seventeenth century probably consisted of yards in which livestock were tethered.  In 1837 Map III shows the shape of these plots on Market Street, whereas the plots on Wood Street are more rectangular, and Ashby Green seems to consist entirely of terraced cottages.  The frontages of the Market Street properties rarely stretch less than twenty feet, and rarely more than 35, with a depth of about 300 feet, making these plots comparable with Totnes where the characteristic house plot measured 20 feet by 300 - 400 feet.[5]

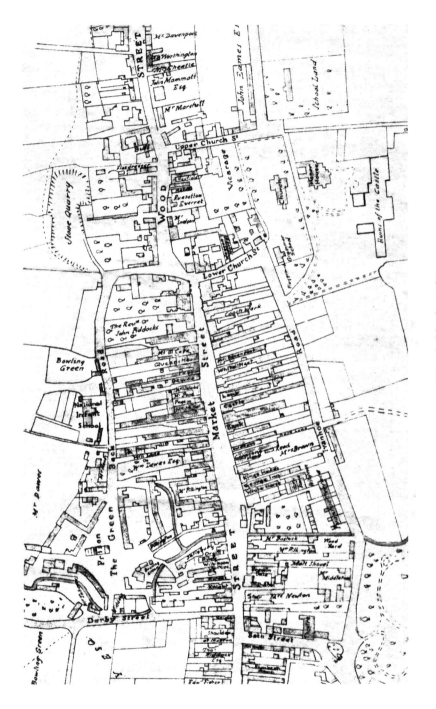

Map III – Ashby in 1837

Aerial view – Market Street from the west
The Castle and St Helen's Church are in the top right section
This photograph dates from the 1940s.
*Courtesy of Ashby Museum*

# TWO

## *Mediaeval Ashby*

IT is convenient to begin with the town's name. The 'de-la-Zouch' suffix differentiated the town from three other Ashbys in Leicestershire, and referred to the fact that for 200 years from the end of the twelfth century the la Souche family were lords of the manor. The 'by' in the name is of Scandinavian origin, and the 'Ash' was derived either from the Anglo-Saxon for an ash-tree, or from an Anglo-Saxon name, such as Aesc or Oisc. Since most of the names of the villages in this area are of Scandinavian origin, it is probable that this area was first intensively settled only after the Scandinavian invasions.

One other place-name within Ashby parish may be mentioned here, as it presents a problem of derivation. The earliest mention of the name 'Callis' that has so far been found is in a land deed dated 1441/2.[1] This refutes Nichols' suggestion that the name 'Callis' owed its origin to the Hastings' connection with Calais[2], for the Hastings family had no interests in Ashby until twenty years later. Mr. Cox of the Place-Names Society has suggested that 'Callis' may have been derived either from 'coal-leys' - although no coal is known to have been found in this area - or, more probably, 'kale-leys' or the cabbage-fields.

The first documentary evidence for the existence of the town is in the Domesday Book, where the inhabitants of 'Ascebi' were listed as two bondmen, a priest, six sokemen, eight villeins and four bordars. The wood in the town was described as measuring one league (1½ miles) long and four furlongs wide, and was sufficient for one hundred pigs. The fourteen yardlands in Ashby had been worth ten shillings before the Conquest, but were, in 1087, worth forty shillings. The

Domesday Book also referred to Alton, which covered 6½ yardlands, Woodcote with two, and Boothorpe with a single ploughland.

Ashby's value of 40 shillings in 1087 had increased by 1337 to a little over £29. Much of this increase in the value of the town was reflected in the increase in population. In 1087 only 21 tenants, including the priest, lived there. By 1377 Ashby contained 223 inhabitants who paid taxes.

Two hundred years later the number of adult males in the town was about 180. Thus, while there was a huge increase in Ashby's population between 1087 and 1377, in the following two centuries there was probably a small reduction. This reduction was probably the result of the Black Death.

The effect of this fall in population may be seen in taxation cuts between 1334 and 1446, and these enable Ashby's position to be compared with that of other Leicestershire towns. In 1334 Ashby was probably the sixth largest town in the county, paying £7-5-0 in tax, whereas Leicester paid over £26, Melton Mowbray - £14, Wigston Magna - £8-8-0, Bottesford - £8-5-0 and Great Bowden - £7-13-4. Ashby in 1324 was therefore larger than either Loughborough or Barrow-on-Soar, which paid less than £7.[3]

By 1446 this position had changed significantly. Leicester and Melton were still the two largest towns, although their taxes had been cut by 21% and 38% respectively. Wigston was now taxed at £5-5-0, a cut of 40%, and Barrow's taxation had been reduced by 47%. Yet Loughborough, less than five miles from Barrow, had had its taxes cut by only 2.5%, and had emerged as the most important economic centre in the north of the county. Ashby's tax had been cut by 7%, and it was still therefore one of the most important half dozen towns in the county.[4]

Roger la Souche established the right to hold an annual fair in Ashby in 1219 on the even and feast day of St. Helen (August 18th), the patronal saint of the parish church. A market every Wednesday was established at the same time, but in 1261 Alan la Souche was granted the right to hold a market at Ashby every Saturday, in lieu of the market that had been held on Tuesdays. The original market day, therefore, seems to have been changed twice within its first fifty years.

The early markets included, no doubt, the retailing of all manner of provisions but wool was not one of the principal commodities of the town. In 1260 Leicester Corporation listed eight places where the *'foreign'* merchant was able to buy wool in the county but these did not include Ashby. Ashby farmers in the 17th century concentrated upon cattle rather than sheep, and there is one indication that leather was also an important product in earlier centuries. A charter from the middle of the twelfth century mentioned the land of *'Hakon the sutor'*, or 'shoemaker'.[5] It is significant that, although Hakon held land, he used shoe-making as the description of his occupation. It is also significant that Hakon, the shoemaker, was important enough to warrant a separate mention in this charter.

There are few signs that the establishment of a market and fair in Ashby a century after this charter brought immediate prosperity to the town. In 1337 an *Inquisition post mortem* of William la Souche valued the market with the fair as being worth only 12/- a year out of his total annual income from the town of £29-1-4.[6] At a similar time an *Inquisition post mortem* of Henry de Beaumont showed that the Loughborough fairs and markets were valued at £5 a year, and the income from the fair alone at Leicester was 24/- a year.[7]

A century later, in 1403, the market at Ashby was small enough to be stopped by three men. Sir Hugh Burnell accused Robert Goos, John Howe and John Fisscher of Ashby of having *'with threats attacked those men who came near there [Ashby] with their victuals and other things to buy and sell, so that for a long time they were afraid to come, to the great damage of the said Hugh Burnell'.*[8]

Although the fact that Ashby had markets and fairs may have enabled it to recover its economic strength after the Black Death more quickly than purely agricultural villages, the expansion of the town between 1087 and 1403 does not appear to have owed much to the town's right to hold markets and fairs.

An *Inquisition post mortem* of 1347[9] mentioned *'the dwelling house (mansum) of the manor'*, which indicates that some of the la Souche family probably resided in the town. But this family was not particularly rich, owning, apart from Ashby, only one other manor, in Cambridgeshire. Nor did they play any notable part in national politics.

For sixty years after the death of the last la Souche the ownership of the manor was disputed. It fell into the hands of James Butler, Earl of Ormond, a leading supporter of Henry VI, but at the battle of Towton, he was taken prisoner, and later beheaded. In February 1461/2 Edward IV granted the manor of Ashby to the family who were to be the last manorial lords of the town - the Hastings.

This grant proved a turning-point in the town's history. The Earl of Ormond had been a man of national importance, as was Lord Hastings. But it is not clear if the Earl visited Ashby and his connection with the town was brief. For the next two hundred years the Hastings family continued to be active in national politics, and to maintain Ashby as their main seat.

The most tangible indication of their connection with the town was the castle. Some parts of the castle date from the twelfth century. By the fifteenth century, after years of Civil War, it was rare for the king to allow his subjects to build fortified homes – only five were licensed by Edward IV. In 1474, however, this king gave Lord Hastings permission to build houses in his manors of Kirby, Thornton and Bagworth and to erect a fortified manor-house in Ashby.

Some of the existing castle was rebuilt, and a great deal was added to it. The four-storied tower that once formed the principal living quarters of the Hastings family and part of which still stands, suggests the strength of the building (see page 27). In the Civil War the castle withstood a siege of sixteen months.

At the same time as Lord Hastings was licensed to build Ashby castle he was also given permission to enclose and impark 3,000 acres in Ashby. One park had existed in Ashby for several centuries but it was, apparently, like the old castle, regarded as inadequate for the new family. The imparking of this land will be discussed later. What is important in this context is that these licences to build a castle and impark this land suggest that the Hastings family had already decided to make Ashby their seat.

What were the immediate economic effects upon the town of the residence of so powerful a family? One immediate effect relates to the rebuilding of the castle and, at the same time the substantial rebuilding of St Helen's Parish Church. When Lord Hastings built his house at Kirby Muxloe, about eighteen miles to the south-east of Ashby, his warden was John Lyle, of Ashby.[10] *Le ffreston'* for Kirby was quarried at Alton, and the lead for the roof was bought *'by the hands of Rob[er]t Wodhous at Assheby'*,[11] even though the lead itself came from Wirksworth in Derbyshire. So Lord Hastings chose to use an Ashby trader for his lead purchases, even though Leicester was considerably nearer to Kirby.

Unfortunately the accounts for the building of Ashby castle and St Helen's do not survive. But it seems likely that the stone for the castle and the church was quarried locally. If Lord Hastings used an Ashby man as his warden at Kirby, he probably used other local people in similar positions at Ashby. Though the engineers were, no doubt, experts brought in from outside the town, the labourers were probably local men. Moreover, the feeding and equipping of these workers must have brought business to many inhabitants of the town who were not directly involved with the construction.

Another immediate economic consequence of the Hastings' adoption of the town as their main seat was the addition of an extra fair, for Lord Hastings secured the grant of two fairs at Ashby. One of these was on the eve of Pentecost (Whitsunday) and for four days afterwards, and the other on the eve of St. Simon and St. Jude (October 28th) and for four days afterwards. The fairs that were granted then continued to be held on these dates for at least two hundred years. In 1613 a petition was lodged to augment these with new fairs on Easter Tuesday and St. Matthew's Day (September 21st), but the licence granted in 1617 allowed new fairs on Easter Tuesday and St. Bartholomew's Day (August 24th). These four fairs were still being held on the same days in 1675.[12]

It must also be noted that these fairs lasted much longer than their predecessors. The 1219 grant allowed a fair to be held on two successive days, but in 1337 the fair seems to have lasted only one day. Lord Hastings secured fairs for ten days every year.

The residence of a powerful lord such as Lord Hastings must also have provided many new opportunities for local traders and farmers. In 1564 the Earl's household consisted of 77 servants[13] – all of whom required feeding, as well as livery and shoes to wear.

The first reference to trading activities occurs in 1489 when one leather-worker, John Barker, was fined for selling unfit leather,[14] at the same time 38 inhabitants of Ashby were punished for failing to keep the assize of ale. All 38 were women, which suggests that the brewing of ale was regarded as a woman's work. As trade increased during the next two hundred years more men became involved with the opening of alehouses, and the provision of food and lodging for travellers. By the end of the seventeenth century innkeeping had not merely become a respectable occupation, but most of the leading men in the town were engaged in it.

In 1489 five men were punished for offending against the assize of bread, and the coroners of the market - the earliest mention of such officers in Ashby - also prosecuted a man for selling bad fish.

Hastings Tower, Ashby Castle
*Courtesy of Lara Peach*

These references suggest that, by the end of the fifteenth century, many of the inhabitants of Ashby were becoming reliant on trade as well as agriculture. A century later it would not have been worth increasing the numbers of fairs if it had not been felt that there was enough trade to justify ten days a year.

The principal occupation of Ashby people in the years immediately after the arrival of the Hastings, however, continued to be agriculture. As can be seen in Map II, there were three town fields: – the Great Field to the north; the Middle Field to the West (spanning the modern Moira Road and Burton Road); and the Lionswell Field to the southwest. These were divided into strips and, as we shall see, the town rules were very clear about how each resident must not farm in a way that caused problems for his neighbours.

The town operated within a feudal system, with the lords of the manor at the apex. Different classes of townsfolk, with different rights and responsibilities lived below him, but all of them were liable to do a certain number of days working for the lord each year.

Between 1374 and 1570 few documents indicate the social or economic changes in the town. But by 1570 Ashby had a population of about 800. It was a small, if thriving, market town which still depended to a considerable extent upon agriculture. Socially it was dominated by the manorial power of the Hastings family, the head of which had, in 1529, been given the title of Earl of Huntingdon. But over the next century and a half much of this was to change. By 1720 the manorial lord no longer lived in the town, and some of his economic influence had disappeared. Over this period the population of Ashby had doubled, and, by 1720, the majority of the population was primarily dependent upon trade and manufactures. Moreover by 1720 the 'golden age' of the small market town had passed. The following chapters will be concerned with tracing the period first of prosperity, and then of decline in this town.

St Helen's Parish Church and its fifteenth century sun-dial
*Courtesy of Ashby Museum*

# THREE

## *Demography*

BETWEEN 1567 and 1580 the average number of baptisms in Ashby each year was 26.5. Adopting Professor Hoskins' method of calculation[1], this would indicate a total population at this time of 800 people – or about 180 households. This suggests that Ashby at this time was the third largest town in the county. Leicester remained the largest with 600 households while Loughborough had a little over 250. Lutterworth recorded 106, Shepshed 103 and Hinckley 100. Of the large towns of the early fourteenth century, before the Black Death, Melton Mowbray, Great Bowdon and Wigston each had 80 households in 1563, while Bottesford had only seventy.

In 1603 *Liber Cleri* recorded that the number of communicants in Ashby was 700. Using once again Hoskins' suggestion that non-communicants (mainly children under 15) formed about 40% of the total population, the total population of Ashby in 1603 was a little under 1,200.[2] Between 1601 and 1620 the average number of baptisms each year was 37.8, suggesting a total population of just over 1,100.

The 1676 Compton census and the Hearth Tax assessments of 1670 both suggest that the total population at that time was also just below 1,200. In 1705, Bishop Wake's survey of his diocese stated that there were 300 families in Ashby,[3] which indicates that there were then 1,350 inhabitants.

All these estimates from different sources paint a consistent picture. By the beginning of the seventeenth century, Ashby's population had increased by about 50% from its total fifty years previously. It remained at a level of 1,200 for most of the seventeenth century; but by the early eighteenth century it was starting to increase again.

This does not mean that the seventeenth century was a time of demographic stability. The period immediately before the Civil War seems to have been a time of population growth. In 1638 Humphrey Kirke submitted to the Earl of Huntingdon a list of *'all the new errected houses in Ashbye'*.[4] This list detailed 39 houses. Even though Humphrey Kirke did not define what he meant by *'new'* and some of the houses may have been rebuilding of older properties, it seems clear that in the years before 1638 there had been a significant expansion in housing to cope with increased population. Immediately after the Civil War the numbers of baptisms and marriages drop, which suggests a decline in overall numbers in the 1650s and 1660s. The numbers of baptisms and marriages suggest there was renewed growth in the last decades of the century.

The parish registers can provide more sophisticated information than simple totals of baptisms, marriages and burials. Of the 86 men whose birth and marriage dates are both known, the average age at marriage was 27.3 years. Of a similar sample of 137 women, the average age was 26.7 years. The sample is too small to indicate any changes during the course of the century, but only two men and one woman first married when they were over 45, and only eight women and one man when they were less than 20 years old. This reinforces the argument that in this period marriages only took place when the man was able to establish his own household and support himself.[5]

The three largest families during this century numbered 10, 11, and 14. The family of fourteen included two sets of twins. The average number of children in each family was five. Again there is no significant difference between the results obtained for the various periods.

These statistics have to be treated with caution. They are based on reconstituting families from the parish registers, but do not take into account families that moved into or out of the town. How great was the volume of this migration in Ashby? The parish registers suggest that several families left Ashby during, or immediately after, the Civil War.

To take one example, there were 21 families that were called Ash or Ashe between 1570 and 1645. Between 1645 and 1720 there were only eight. Two of these seem to have been re-marriages, so that there were probably only six Ashe households during this period. Two of these may not even have lived in the parish. John Ash was married in Ashby in 1656, but had no children baptised in the town, nor were he or his wife buried there. Another Ash, Thomas, was known well enough in the town for his marriage at Measham to be recorded in the Ashby register; but again no children of this marriage were baptised at Ashby. Only one Ash family was started before, and certainly remained in the parish after, 1645.

The parish registers also indicate that the rate of infant mortality – where the child died within a year of birth - varied between 100 and 120 per 1,000. The mortality rate was better for children who survived their first year, but the parish registers still suggest that over a quarter of children died before reaching their fifth birthday.

Of the 2,000 or so families where the place of residence at the time of marriage is known, the overwhelming majority, 1,766, came from within the parish. 322 listed other parishes and 313 of those came from identifiable places. Out of this 313, 247 (79%) travelled less than ten miles.

The wills of Ashby people in this period demonstrate a desire to preserve the family property as a single entity. As long as the needs of adult dependants for life, and of minor dependants until they reached their majority, had been satisfied, then a single person, usually the eldest son, would inherit the property.

Out of 348 wills that were made between 1570 and 1720, 246 (71% of all wills) left the bulk of the property either to a single person, or to two people of whom one was the deceased's wife, or occasionally, his mother. While many such wills left a share in the property to the deceased's wife for her lifetime, the property, after the wife's death, was usually then inherited by a single person.

In only 15% of all wills was the property divided. In just 25 wills (7% of all wills) the property was divided into more than two parts. But in the vast majority of Ashby wills during this period the property was intended to be inherited by a single person, who was, usually, the eldest son of the deceased.

Of course, the mortality rates meant that most wills were necessarily filled with provisos depending on who might still be alive to inherit the property. The health of individuals in society was a matter of considerable importance to neighbours as well as to family members. The Overseers of the Poor and the Churchwardens, as we shall see, made special provision for people who were sick to be looked after by their neighbours, or by adults who were skilled in health care.

There are few references to the cause of death in the parish registers or in other documents, although there is one reference to *'a poore vagrant that was visited grievously with the small pox'*.[6]

But clearly the most feared illness was the plague, which could wipe out whole families in a short space of time. In 1602/3 John Brinsley noted in one of his devotional works, that the town was afflicted with plague.[7] In 1609 the parish registers recorded the death of *'a strainger which disessed in Callys suspected to dy of the plage'*. In 1610 the plague raged in Leicester prompting John Burrowes, on the Earl of Huntingdon's behalf, to appeal to the mayor of Leicester *'that none of your towne...should repayre to the fayre of Ashbey'*.[8] In 1625 rumours that Ashby was suffering from the plague had such a devastating impact on the town's trade that Arthur Hildersham and nine other leading townspeople wrote to the mayor and corporation of Leicester to deny the rumours.[9] In 1627 the Churchwardens paid three shillings for *'pooder for anie that might be infect with ye plage'*.[10] In 1631 the plague was '*much raging*' in this part of Leicestershire.[11] In the late summer of 1645, the sixty men left to defend Ashby castle in the Civil War were stricken by plague which forced them out of the castle buildings, and the besiegers in Coleorton withdrew to Leicester in fear of catching it themselves.[12] Samuel Shaw, schoolmaster in Ashby from 1668/9 to 1695, lost two of his children, two friends and a servant to the plague in the 1660s.[13] In 1671 the school accounts noted that only two feoffees were living, '*the rest being dead suddenly of the plague*'.[14] This incidence of plague at least nine times in the space of 90 years is comparable with Cambridge where plague struck ten times in sixty years.[15]

For many people, life in the seventeenth century was short.

# FOUR

# *Trade*

## I. OCCUPATIONAL STRUCTURE BEFORE THE CIVIL WAR

IN April 1637 the vicar of Ashby started to record the occupations of all men who were mentioned in the parish registers. It is not clear why he began to do this. The vicar, Anthony Watson, had already served the parish for at least 12 years. But for a few years on the eve of the Civil War, the parish registers provide the most accurate record of the occupational structure of the town.

Of the 221 men whose occupations were listed in the parish registers between 1637 and 1640: 34% (76) listed their primary occupation as being agricultural (labourers, husbandmen, yeomen and shepherd or swineherd); 22% (49) were involved in the leather industry (shoemakers, translators i.e. cobblers, fellmongers, glovers, tanners, saddlers, whittawers and curriers); 9% (19) were in the building trade (carpenters, joiners, glaziers, tilers, masons and plasterer); 8% (17) were either tailors or weavers and 5% (12) were traders, such as mercers, chapmen or carriers. 17% (37) were of other occupations – including five blacksmiths, three maltsters, two wheelwrights and two ploughwrights.

The jobs listed in the "agricultural" section need some further explanation. 'Labourer' may have been more a description of a man's social position than his occupation, but it did not necessarily reflect a poor man. Leonard Trenthom, who died in 1638, called himself a labourer, and left £35-15-0. Richard Vinson who died in 1660 was also called a labourer and left almost £33. George Swindell, another labourer, was assessed in 1663 at four hearths, and in 1666 at five. 'Labourers' were men who did not primarily occupy themselves with trade or exercise a specific craft, and therefore probably worked most of the time in agriculture.

A "Yeoman" was not always well off. Ralph Meacock, yeoman, died in 1668 leaving only £26, and had been assessed in 1663 at two hearths. Other yeomen died in the town leaving only fourteen pounds, or less. There were only three 'Yeomen' in this sample, and their inclusion in the "agricultural" section does not make a significant difference to these figures.

The population in 1640 was probably over 1,200, which indicates 280 - 300 households. The list of 221 men in the parish registers, therefore, represents three-quarters of the adult male population.

It must, however, be emphasised that the occupational descriptions given in these registers are not definitive. The numbers who changed their occupational 'tag' was small, but many men were involved in more than one enterprise.

For example, a petition of 1627 referred to the number of ale-houses in the town, as being *'in number more then fortie'*.[1] This number cannot have been greatly exaggerated since the document went on to list 27 alehouses which it concluded were *'fittest to be continewed'*. Yet in the registers between 1637 and 1640 no ale-housekeeper was recorded and there was only one vintner and one distiller of 'strong water'.

The keeping of an ale-house was probably regarded as a subsidiary occupation. A petition from the parishioners of Rugeley a few years earlier[2] complained that traders had established alehouses, and had then begun to neglect their trades and, when their alehouses had failed, had turned to beggary.

In a small community like Ashby, it is unlikely that many men were fulltime traders or craftsmen. Most men, at this time, owned some livestock, and everyone, probably, had some share in the agricultural economy of the town, even if they regarded their primary occupation as being non-agricultural.

For example, Humphrey Kirke, almost certainly the man who compiled the list of *'new errected houses'* mentioned earlier, was an alehouse keeper according to the petition of 1627, but in a deposition in 1638[3] described himself as a carpenter. He worked as a carpenter for the Grammar School in 1620,[4] and was consistently described as a carpenter in the parish registers. In 1615 he held a cottage for three lives with commoning rights for two beasts and fifteen sheep.[5]

Later in the century, John Elton variously described himself as an innkeeper, a dyer or a sharman, and, in 1718, he was the Earl of Huntingdon's most important tenant, paying £90 a year in rent.[6]

Many families continued in the same trades for several generations. Thus the Byard family were cutlers in the town for some fifty years, and successive Caseys were vintners during the seventeenth century. Both the sons of Samuel Smith, glazier, also became glaziers. When the son did not follow his father's trade he often followed an allied trade. For example, Abraham Ashe, son of William Ashe, a tanner, became a shoe-maker in Ashby, and John Hassard, ironmonger, was the son of Thomas Hassard, chandler.

One notable omission from the occupations listed in the parish registers is of colliers. Only one such man appears. Ashby was in the centre of coalfields. Coal had been mined near Coleorton since the twelfth century. The Hastings' mine at Oakthorpe was certainly open in the first half of the century. Perhaps these mines were too far from Ashby or the colliers may have been listed in the registers as 'labourers'.

Ashby's involvement in the leather industry is clear. 22% of the parish register list of occupations related to the leather industry and this is comparable with 23% in Northampton in the early sixteenth century, and 19% of Leicester freemen during the sixteenth century.[7] The leather industry is more usually associated with larger towns, but a fifth of the adults in a small market town, such as Ashby, were leather-workers.

How far was Ashby's participation in the leather industry of more than local importance? In 1600 a dispute arose between the glovers of Mountsorrel, who claimed that they were unfairly excluded from Leicester markets, and Leicester Corporation. The Earl of Huntingdon appeared to be ready to champion his Mountsorrel tenants, and so Robert Herrick wrote to the Leicester Mayor that *'yf yow will strik of that string to offar my lord favor for Ashbye gloovars, which I think will silldom trobell us'* [8] then the Corporation could continue to exclude the men of Mountsorrel. The outcome of this letter is not known, nor is it clear whether Herrick considered that the Ashby glovers would *'silldom trobell us'* because they were twice as far from Leicester as Mountsorrel was, or if he believed that the Ashby glovers were too few, or too poor in their craftsmanship, to cause the Leicester glovers any difficulty.

One other document relating to the interests in trade of Ashby and Leicester is equally ambiguous. In 1613 Ashby asked Leicester and four other market towns for permission to increase the number of fairs held at Ashby from four to six. Leicester Corporation replied that: *'We doe herebye certifie and Signifie that the increase of faiors theire as ys above specified will not bee anie waye preiudiciall or hurtfull unto us in our Markitts or faiors but rather verie beneficiall and Comodiouse by the increase of our trade and trafique and the greater and better vent of our wars comodities and Cattles.'* [9]

There are several possible explanations for this response. More fairs may indeed have increased trade generally. Leicester Corporation may have genuinely felt that such fairs would be in no way *'preiudiciall or hurtfull'* because Ashby was too small and its attraction for traders insignificant. Or, simply, Leicester Corporation may have agreed to the new fairs to avoid offending the Earl.

The Leicester Borough Records are full of references to the Corporation's attempts to ensure the Earl's support. When the Earl had been irritated, the Corporation went to some lengths in trying to placate him. For example, in 1607 they sent to Ashby a gelding as a gift for the Countess. When she refused it, the Corporation kept their messenger with the horse at Ashby for several months, in the hope that she might relent.[10]

The influence of the Hastings family upon the life of Ashby will be discussed more fully in the final chapter. But it must be noted here that the Earls boosted the economy of the town in many ways apart from the addition of new fairs. Although the Earls had to spend much time away, the family estates remained centred upon Ashby, and it was there that they entertained, at great expense, King James I in 1617 and King Charles I seventeen years later.

The household expenses of the family, even when its head was absent, were large. The third Earl maintained a household of 77 servants and most of these lived in or near the castle. In 1609 the rules for the household were laid down very clearly. The Earl's *'expresse commandment is, that no officer or servaunt in [his] house shall (without the knowledge or consent of some of the head officers) use any chare folkes; but that all thinges which are to bee doone shalbe performed by his household servants'.[11]*

But the household could not be entirely self-sufficient. For example, the Earl had to order that no *'laundres'* came directly to the castle *'to fetch any shirtes or lynnen'*, but that each member of his household made private arrangements with local washerwomen.

The extent to which the Hastings family and their servants used local traders and craftsmen is not clear, for the household accounts rarely specify the origin of traders from whom goods were bought. But there are some entries which show that washerwomen were not the only Ashby people to benefit from the Hastings household.

In 1629 the bailiff noted the buying of *'cart clouth & neles'* from Sherwood of Ashby, and *'three cowt fellies'* (wheel-rims) from the Ashby wheelwright. Ashby carriers conveyed goods and money to wherever the Earl was staying. William Adcock of Ashby was duly paid for *'honey and one brewinge of braggit spice'*. £47-3-11 was paid to Abraham

Casey, the Ashby vintner; £8 worth of carpentry was done by Edward Woodcocke; and three receipts, totalling over £30, recorded wares bought from John Armston, a mercer.[12] In the 1640s Nathaniel Bryan, an Ashby baker, was supplying bread to the castle three or four times every week.[13]

Most lords of the manor probably traded with their tenants, for it was good business sense to keep the tenants prosperous in order to enable rents to be collected promptly. But not all lords of the manor resided in the town, or were as wealthy and possessed as much influence as the Hastings family.

The victualling of men sent by Leicester, and presumably elsewhere, to beg favours, or present gifts to the family, must have profited several alehouses. And it must be noted that when the 1627 petition to suppress some of the Ashby alehouses was received by Quarter sessions, the J.P.s resolved that they should do nothing until they had asked for help of the Earl of Huntingdon, *'by reason of his great care w[hi]ch he hath of the good gov[ernmen]t of ye Cuntry in all causes and the rather in respecte of his beinge Lord of the said Towne And of his muche residence there'.* [14]

The fact that the town contained forty alehouses, even if most of these were owned by part-time ale-housekeepers operating mainly on market days, is indicative of Ashby's importance as a local trading centre. St. Albans in 1630 contained 30 inns.[15] The inns or alehouses acted not only as social centres, where news and various types of information were disseminated, and as places of rest for travellers, but also as administrative centres. In about 1690 the Courts of Pie Powder, which decided disputes arising from trading at fairs, were held at the Rose and Crown, and the manorial court was held in the same place in later years.[16]

Inns and ale-houses were also undoubtedly used as meeting places for traders and hence as places of business. In 1673 the manorial court made a specific order prohibiting corn from being sold in public or private houses.[17]

The reasons given in 1627 for proposing the suppression of the Ashby alehouses are noteworthy. *'Divers'* of these alehouses were *'not fitt for entertaynem[en]t in respecte of their povertie their ill scituacon beinge farr from the markett place and the ill condicion of the Alehowsekeepers themselves as well in maynteyneinge drunkennes as in lodginge of Rogues and evill disposed p[er]sons.'*

This petition may have been maliciously drawn up by the alehousekeepers *'fittest to be continewed'* in an attempt to rid themselves of their competitors. But it is interesting that *'beinge farr from the markett place'* was regarded as being such a threat to the market (presumably by encouraging private trading and thus avoiding the market tolls) that it was included in this list.

In the first forty years of the seventeenth century Ashby was a place of some importance as it was the seat of the Earls of Huntingdon; it contained a significant and varied number of traders and its market seems to have thrived. But all this was thrown into jeopardy by the outbreak of Civil War.

## II: AFTER THE CIVIL WAR

### i. The immediate impact of the Civil War

Although the sixth Earl remained nominally neutral, he did not prevent his brother, Lord Loughborough, from taking over the castle at Ashby and garrisoning it on behalf of the King. A Royalist, Richard Symonds, stated in his diary that there were six hundred soldiers in the Ashby garrison.[18] Lord Thomas Grey, leading the local Parliamentarian forces, reported that the Ashby garrison numbered about four hundred,[19] and at the surrender of the castle 300 arms were seized.[20] To secure provisions for this garrison a local man, Ambrose Pemberton of Blackfordby, was appointed Chief Commissary.[21]

Ashby might have profited from the Civil War, and for a time trade seems to have continued. The County Committee later reported that they had received *'informations against some of the best tradesmen in Leicester about their trading with the enemy at Ashby'* during the war.[22] These traders' explanation that they had not realized that the men to whom they had sold provisions were soldiers was not credible, the Committee concluded. In 1645 Thomas Davenport of Hinckley was fined £20 for selling wine to the besieged.[23]

But the overall economic effect of the Civil War upon Ashby was disastrous. First, the Ashby garrison was apparently slow in paying for what was supplied to them. Almost thirty years later the heirs of Ambrose Pemberton were still in dispute with the heirs of Henry Sykes of Ashby, who had supplied the garrison with *'foure fatt oxen and some other fatt cattle Corne and Provisions by him then estimated at seaventy four pounds'* for which he never received more than £30.[24] Pemberton himself had lent money to the garrison.[25]

In this area the war was characterised by small parties of soldiers marauding and looting property. Even before the war, in July 1640, it was reported that some soldiers, while marching to their rendezvous in the North, *'broke into the Earl of Huntingdon's Park at Ashby, where they killed all the white deer, but could not kill the other deer, being more wild.'* [26]

During the war both sides displayed a similar attitude. The Parliamentarians complained that the Ashby garrison *'very much spoil the country .... imprisoning and ransoming the men'*, and were thus proving a *'great annoyance to five counties'.*[27] On the Royalist side, Mr. Symonds recorded in his diary for January 1646 that one Saturday night *'came a party of horse and dragoons into the towne of Ashby, plundered the mercers', sadlers', and sutlers' shopps and the inns of the horses.'* [28] As we shall see, at least fourteen houses in Ashby were *'pulld downe'* during the Civil War.

Trade cannot have flourished in this situation, and even if it continued in some fashion during the period when the castle was under siege, it seems to have been stopped by an outbreak of plague in the summer of 1645.

Most importantly, the castle's success in withstanding the Parliamentarian besiegers for sixteen months resulted in its defences being demolished. The family fortunes were so impaired by the war that in 1653, the sixth Earl of Huntingdon, while still protesting that it had been his brother not he who had been a Royalist, was thrown into the Fleet prison as a common debtor.[29] When the Hastings' fortunes were to some extent repaired by the Restoration of the monarchy, their home at Ashby was uninhabitable and the family moved to Castle Donington, about nine miles away. The primary interest of the family in the economic welfare of the town, and the direct economic stimulus of the residence of the family in Ashby therefore ended.

The departure of the Hastings may have led to a drift away from Ashby of able-bodied men in search of work. In the 1676 Census of communicants, there was an imbalance of 299 males to 379 females.[30]

Finally it must also be noted that, although only just over 10% of Lord Loughborough's forces were local men[31], some of these were disabled as a result of their fighting. In 1684 it was recorded at quarter sessions that Richard Cheatle of Ashby, husbandman *'did serve His Late Ma[jes]tie as a Souldier in the late Civill wars under the Comand of the right hon[our]able the Lord of Loughborow...and yt he did behave himselfe couragiously & faithfully and was very much wounded by reason whereof......he is very much disabled and become very poore'.*[32] Cheatle was only awarded a pension at this time, almost forty years after the siege of Ashby, because Eaglesfield, another old soldier of Ashby, and a previous pensioner, had recently died.

*ii. Changes in occupational structure after the Civil War.*

The longer term effects of the Civil War upon occupational structure within the town are difficult to analyse, as there is no listing of occupations comparable with the data supplied by the parish registers between 1637 and 1643.

Inventories suggest that in the second half of the century there was a shift away from the preoccupation with agriculture which was characteristic of the earlier period. In the period before 1645 76% or more of the surviving inventories included some livestock. In the fifty years from 1670 the corresponding percentage was 64%.

70% of the less wealthy owned cattle before 1645, whereas this declined to about 45% after 1645. The comparable figures for sheep owners showed a decline from over 30% to just over 20%. There is no evidence that this shift away from the ownership of livestock was balanced by an increase in the arable land farmed by these men.

Such a shift away from agriculture does not, of course, imply that trade was flourishing. As we shall see, it probably was not. But when men were forced to choose between their different interests, they tended, or were forced, to cut back on their stake in agriculture.

There were attempts to establish hosiery manufacture in Ashby early in the eighteenth century. Joseph Canner and his wife moved from Melton Mowbray to Ashby in 1715[33] and this man died 25 years later leaving a shop of frames, including five stocking frames.[34] Thomas Nash, *'framework knitter'* from Middlesex came to the town in 1700, John Bailey *'stuff weaver'* from Coleorton in 1716, William Walker *'framework knitter'* from Breadsall in Derbyshire in 1719, and in the same year Thomas Moore and family, a *'tammy weaver'*, arrived from Coventry. Work of this kind had probably been carried on in the town in a small way for generations, but this sudden influx of workers suggests that there was a concerted attempt to found a new industry in the town at this time. John Taylor of Ashby was in 1692 given a little over £2/10/0 by the Wright charity to buy twenty wheels, five reels

Ashby Castle in ruins after the western wall of the Kitchen Tower (left of picture) and the southern wall of the Hastings Tower (foreground) were demolished.
*Courtesy of Ashby Museum*

and some spindles. The town charity may have thought it worthwhile to sponsor new industry that might reduce the numbers of poor. In 1795 Sir Frederick Morton Eden was able to describe the inhabitants of Ashby not only as innkeepers, shopkeepers, farmers and labourers, but also as *'Manufacturers of woollen and cotton stockings, and hats'*.[35]

Eden's reference to innkeepers confirms the continuing importance to the Ashby economy of travellers. This interest may have been declining, however, for in 1795 the number of alehouses was reduced from 25 to 21, compared with about forty in 1627 when the town's population was about half the size. By way of contrast, in Loughborough in 1770 there were 43 inns and alehouses, and thirteen years later 50.[36]

A census was taken in 1686 of the number of guest beds and the numbers of horses that could be stabled.[37] The figures for Ashby were 138 and 278 respectively. Leicester could accommodate far more travellers than any other town in the county, with space for 578 guests and 1,143 horses. Only four other towns in the county could accommodate more than 100 visitors. Loughborough had 121 guest beds and had stabling for 172 horses, although this latter figure may have been incorrect, as inns usually accommodated two horses for each person. Hinckley, in the south of the county, could accommodate 130 guests and 358 horses; Melton Mowbray, to the north-east of Leicester, 113 guests and 341 horses; and Market Harborough, to the south-east 107 guests and 218 horses. This suggests that Ashby was still one of six local trading centres.

*iii. Changes in the market economy of Ashby 1640-1720.*

At the beginning of the eighteenth century we are able to judge, for the first time, the range of influence of Ashby's markets and fairs, when the homes of butchers and bakers who visited Ashby market were recorded by the manorial court.

In the court records surviving for the period 1707-1714[38] 52% of the bakers and 36% of the butchers trading in Ashby lived elsewhere. Butchers came from twenty two other villages or towns, and bakers from fourteen other places. For both trades, half came from villages within a five mile radius and the remainder travelled between five and fifteen miles.

A list of all the horses bought and sold at the horse fair in 1697 gives an indication of the influence of the fairs, although it is not clear whether this fair was typical.[39] A total of 16 horses were sold, at prices ranging from 13/- to £4-1-0. Buyers and sellers came from seven different counties. Altogether 26 men were listed from 22 different places. Six men came from less than five miles away. A further six travelled between five and fifteen miles, and eight travelled more than fifteen miles. Six place names have not been identified.

In general it seems clear that the markets attracted people from up to fifteen miles away, whereas the fairs attracted some people from 40-50 miles, although the majority still travelled less than twenty miles.

How far were the markets and fairs prospering in this period? By 1653 the markets at Ashby had been re-established in the town[40] and the fact that in the 1650s and 1660s several traders were manufacturing their own tokens, suggests that trade was sufficiently promising for such an expensive operation to be thought worthwhile. Seven traders were presented at the manorial court in 1667 for issuing these brass halfpence.[41] Four of these were mercers, one described himself as an ironmonger, and another as a cordwainer, while the occupation of the last is unknown. At least four other traders also issued their own coins during the 1660s and 1670s. The Red Lion token of 1669 is pictured on page 51.

By the end of the 1660s the correspondence of Mr. Jaques, the Earl of Huntingdon's agent, was filled with tales of poor markets and fairs. In 1667 he reported that '*I was both at Ashby and Lenton faire in hopes to have served my Lady and the Ladys in selling there horses but cold not nothinge went of but good geldinges that were fitt for present service'.*[42] In 1670, *'the faire has been bad'* [43] and at the 1672 fair *'nothing sold well'.*[44] In 1684 *'nothing sells nor tradesmen can worke to gett moneys'.*[45] In the following year *'nothing but what is fitt for the butchers will make moneys: and that gives poor prises.'*[46]

In the same year, John Elton, the bailiff of the market, was reported as saying that *'he had many bad faires; all sorts of goods not selling'.*[47] Of course, these complaints of poor trading may have been simply excuses to explain Mr. Jaques' failure to collect rents on time. Yet, the Earl apparently made no attempt to replace Mr. Jaques by someone more efficient. Mr. Jaques remained in office until his death in 1688, and his reports were echoed by his successor, Mr. Piddocke. In 1689 the latter wrote that *'most ten[an]ts depended on the new Markets and they have failed them and can sell nothing.'* [48] *'The tymes I must confesse have been extreamly bad for poor tenants.'*[49] In the same year he summed up the situation very clearly, *'I was in greate hopes the faire would have filled my empty purses. But...I must confesse it was the worst faire that ever I saw. Nothing sold almost and what did sell went att so lame a Rate that unlesse tymes amend, most ten[a]nts will be undone'.*[50]

The failure of the markets and fairs was reflected by the decline in the rent for the bailiwick of the market. In 1685, Mr. King, the former bailiff, refused to pay £32 again for this office, but offered £28.[51] Finally John Elton took it at a rent of £30 a year,[52] but in 1688 would offer only £25 a year, claiming that the previous year he had been a *'great loser by the bailywick'.*[53] The following year Mr. Piddocke *'with much adoe settled the Bailywick at Ashby w[i]th John Elton att £24 p.a....I was with Mr. King and Mason privately but neither would meddle'.*[54] Thus in seven years the rent of the bailiwick declined by 25%, and while Mr. King had been prepared to take the post at £28 a year in 1683, he would not *'meddle'* with it at £24 in 1689.

The decline in the bailiwick rent and the failure of the markets may have been partly the result of an increase in private trading. The promulgation of a bylaw in 1673 stating that everyone *'shall bring into the open markett all their...corne'*, with a penalty of 4d for every strike that was *'concealed or set up in any publick or private house during the tyme of the Cornemarkitt'* [55] suggests that this was the case. Or, it could be argued, the Earl's tenants were unable to pay their rents because the market had shifted further down the street, away from the Earl's property, as a result of Elton taking the bailiwick. Mr. Jaques certainly feared this: *'If Elton take itt the markett wil be againe removed downe towards the bridge and from amongst yor owne tenants.'* [56]

Much of the decline in prosperity was, no doubt, the result of an agricultural depression, but this was not the only cause. Contemporaries had various explanations. In 1684 the weather was blamed, and in particular it was stated that the mills had been *'locked up with this frost'.*[57] In 1672 Mr. Jaques concluded *This warre with the Dutch makes great distractione amongst us and a deadness of all things'.*[58] In 1686, on the other hand, corn was so cheap that all the bakers and millers wanted reductions in rent, and in particular, John Swaine, one of the Earl's millers, claimed that he had lost £20 in one year from Ashby mills.[59] In 1689 Mr. Piddocke argued that the soldiers in the town were responsible. *'We are so full of soldiers here in private houses, on free quarter, that it putts all things att p[re]sent out of order',*[60] and a few months later wrote that *'if theise souldiers continue here next Easter faire will signify nothing.'*[61]

But apart from these particular causes the absence of the Hastings family must also have contributed to the trading depression. As their presence had certainly stimulated the growth and prosperity of Ashby in the period before the Civil War, so their absence caused stagnation. It is true that it remained in the economic interest of the lord to make his tenants prosperous, and Mr. Piddocke stated in 1690 that *'it hath been and shall be my method to buy all things of your ten[a]nts subject to your provisoe'.*[62] But Ashby was not the only town where most of the inhabitants were tenants of the Earl of Huntingdon.

One further problem which may have aggravated the economic depression in this period relates to the improvement in communications. It is not clear if these improvements were as great as those which renewed the prosperity of Stamford, but it is probable that, unlike Stamford, Ashby stood to lose more than it gained from any improvements in communications.[63] Better communications enabled more people to travel into the larger towns, such as Leicester and Derby, and the local market centres became less important.

One particular aspect of the general economic depression in the second half of the seventeenth century may be noted, namely the failure of the coal mines at Oakthorpe. Accounts in 1606 and 1607 for the Earl's mines show that these were then making a profit.[64] But in 1652 it was reported that the Oakthorpe mines had been closed since the start of the Civil War and they were in financial difficulties almost as soon as they reopened. In the three months from January to March 1667 the value of the coal that was mined was just over £947 and the expenses £362. Yet almost £595 of this coal was not sold.[65] In 1671 4,549 loads of coal were stockpiled, and some of the coal that was sold from this stock had to be sold cheaply as it had been in store for three years. The expenditure on Oakthorpe mines in that year included interest upon a loan of £1,200 and the total deficit on the mines in 1671 was estimated at over £2,000.

Various attempts were made to make them profitable but they seem to have been closed throughout most of the eighteenth century and were re-opened in 1805. It is clear that the Hastings family during the second half of the 17th century did not find them profitable and the fact that the coal, once mined, could not be sold, reflects a general economic depression.

By the 1690s Ashby was no longer the important local centre that it had been before the war. The demolition of the castle effectively destroyed the military, and political, importance of Ashby. But the town could, and did, continue to act as a local trading centre, and its fairs continued to attract men from a wider area.

Front and back of Francis Sikes' Red Lion token of 1669
(Actual size: 20mm diameter)
*Courtesy of Ashby Museum*

# FIVE

## *Social Structure & Poor Relief*

### I. BEFORE THE CIVIL WAR

NO Ashby trader dominated the town in the sixteenth century as William Wigston dominated Leicester. A man who left over £100 in Ashby in the final quarter of the sixteenth century was a rich man, whereas in a large town such as Leicester such wealth was more common.

In Ashby the wealthiest members of the community in the period up to 1645 were involved primarily with agriculture. Of the 44 people whose wealth, according to their inventories, exceeded the equivalent of £50 at the end of the sixteenth century (which equates to £90 by the end of the seventeenth century), the occupations of 32 are known, and a further five were women. Of these 32, four described themselves as husbandmen, one as a farmer, and eight as yeomen. A further four described themselves as gentlemen, two were chandlers and three were mercers. There were also a single tanner, blacksmith, knight, butcher, vintner, cordwainer, shoemaker and currier. The wealthiest man in this period was Arthur Hildersham, vicar of Ashby, who left £535. Anthony Gilby, the Puritan preacher, left £87. The leather industry was well represented with four men connected with leather in this classification.

But it must be emphasised again that these men were not necessarily involved with a single occupation. Although William Smythe was primarily concerned with the leather trade - he left almost £170 worth of leather - he also owned 120 sheep and thirteen cattle.

What of the townspeople who were below the wealthiest class? If we assume that those who did not make wills were in the poorest class, then between 1621 and 1645 9% of Ashby's population fell into the wealthiest class (leaving more than £160), a further 9% possessed moderate wealth (leaving £80-£160); 22% were of modest means (leaving between £24 and £80) and 60% were poor (leaving less than £24). Such figures are comparable with those for Leicester a century earlier, calculated by Professor Hoskins. He concluded that about 60% of Leicester's population were either exempted from taxation or only just qualified. Another 30% represented the lower middle class, 7% the 'solid core of the middle class' and about 3% the comfortably well-off.[1]

The numbers of poor in Ashby in the years immediately before the Civil War can also be examined through the accounts of the Overseers of the Poor, which survive from 1624-1638, and provide a detailed record of the treatment of the poor.[2]

During these years about 230 adults received grants from the Overseers. This total represents about one-third of the population of approximately seven hundred adults.

Although many of these people received grants only a few times during the period, it is also clear that some men and women were dependent on this relief. John Cox received a grant thirty times in 1624, 35 times in the following year and 43 times in 1626. From 1627 until his death in September 1633 he received a grant every week. Richard Godsbey or his wife received relief over 40 times, and usually over fifty times, every year between 1629 and 1637. Richard Huntwicke received grants every week from early in 1625 until the melancholy grant of 2d towards his grave in December 1631.

Grants were intended to supplement the recipients' incomes, rather than to replace them. The standard wage for labourers and ditchers at this time was 8d a day. Grants from the Overseers of the Poor rarely exceeded 8d a week.

The numbers who received poor relief, however, must have kept the Overseers busy. Between 1624 and 1638 the sums paid out varied from £22 to over £40 a year and the Overseers met every week, usually on a Thursday, to dole out their grants.

Most of the Overseers' money was used for the relief of Ashby residents. But some outsiders, particularly ministers approved by the local vicar, were given small grants. In 1624 over 68 people from outside the town were assisted, at a total cost of just over 25/-. This was not an average year. In 1628 £3/7/6 was given to more than 117 outsiders, and in the following year £2/12/0 to more than 143. In 1631 only 32/9 was given to more than 47 people. In 1635 16/5 was granted to outsiders, in 1636 30/1 and in the following year 14/6.

Of these outsiders two groups are noteworthy. In 1628 more than thirty Irishmen, in small groups, were given a total of 17/7 as they passed through Ashby. The following year more than 43 received two shillings and seven pence. After 1629 the number of Irishmen specified in the Poor accounts declined.

There were also several soldiers who received grants. Altogether 229 soldiers received poor relief between 1624 and 1632. Most of these (94) passed through the town in 1628 and 1629. Perhaps economic problems or religious enthusiasm persuaded men to travel and fight abroad, or perhaps the Overseers in these two years were particularly inclined to support such visitors. Many of the soldiers in 1631 were noted as having *'had ye seale of ye K[ing]of Bohemia And of ye Prince of Orange'*, and were therefore involved in the Thirty Years' War. Not all these soldiers were outsiders. In 1624 the Overseers gave a grant to *'yonge Berdsley and Moore when they went into Germany'*, presumably to fight in the war there.

It is worth noting here that these payments were in addition to the accounts and grants made by the churchwardens[3]. The latter collected miscellaneous fines – for example in 1627 2/- was collected by the Constable *'for a man being drunke'*; and 10/- for *'an oth that Abra. Jackson's wife spoke against Abra. Watson'*. These were augmented by small legacies left by townspeople in their will. In addition the Earl of

Huntingdon regularly contributed £2-13-4 each year to these funds and there were also collections in church at Communion services.

The sums collected by the churchwardens were generally spent on appeals from outside the town. For example, in 1633, they gave money to a parish church in Hereford; to individuals who had suffered losses in fires in the Isle of Ely; Little Bisham in Lincolnshire and Newton Colne; and for individuals in Wiltshire, Staffordshire and Nottinghamshire. It is clear that these were all causes that had received the vicar's approval.

But they also gave money for special cases in the town. In the same year, 1633, the churchwardens drew up an agreement to lend 50/- to Mary Goodman of Ashby to enable her to educate, feed, clothe and generally bring up her grandson, John Knight. If she died leaving him chargeable to the town, that is before he was apprenticed, she forfeited her possessions, listed in an inventory and consisting of '*1 brasse pot and a kettle, one cubborde & 2 cofers*'.

The causes for which the grants were made by the Overseers of the Poor were as varied as the size of their grants, but, unlike the Churchwardens, the Overseers concentrated primarily on Ashby's inhabitants.

Not all grants were to relieve poverty in the usual sense. In 1625 oil was purchased for the church bells, and wine was purchased from Abraham Casey for celebrating communion. One shilling a quarter was paid for Simon, the son of Mr. Thomas Perrins, to be taught by Widow Harding. Simon Perrins later became one of the leading feoffees of the Grammar School.

But small sums were given out to poor people regularly every week. At various times the houses of poor people were repaired; poor boys were apprenticed; clothes and coal were provided and in a practical way the Overseers of the Poor tried to set men, and women, on their feet. In 1631 Widow Buckerfield was given a reaping hook, and in

1636 three shillings was paid *for phisicke and dyet for Clarson at what tyme he was hurt by Narborowes boy.'*

Occasionally large grants were made, particularly to help cure the crippled. In 1628 a blind girl and Ann Sansom, who was lame, received a pound in June and a further pound in July. In the same year three shillings was paid towards carrying Ann Sansom to Newark. In 1629 she received a further pound *'towards curing her legg and to carry her up to London'*, and two years later Nathaniel Hildersham, son of the Ashby vicar, was paid £1/3/4, which he had spent in London on behalf of Ann Sansom.

The generosity of the Overseas of the Poor was often matched by the charity of the Hastings family. The Overseers of the Poor frequently distributed gifts to the poor on behalf of the Countess of Huntingdon. But, in addition to the donations to the Churchwardens noted above, the Earl was accustomed to give out money as he travelled about the manor, in what appears to be an indiscriminate fashion. For example, in 1616 his accounts recorded that he had given two pence to a poor man *'in Ashby filds as Y[our]H[onour]came from the pitts'.*[4] Even during the Civil War the Earl continued to be generous. In 1643 John Draper was given sixpence *'to buy him tobacco'* and five shillings was given to *'young firebrasse to buy him an Asse.'*[5] Once it was recorded that, as the Earl came away from the castle, five shillings was dispensed to *'the poore at the gate'.*[6]

But the number of poor people that the town could support was limited. Some inhabitants were bribed to stop appealing for more help, and many times the constable had to drive poor travellers away from the town. Thus in 1627 Isabell Hill was given two shillings: *'shee p[ro]missinge not to com to us for anie more'.* In 1631 1/8 was paid *'for sending away Mary Richardson'.* In 1634 William Tomlinson's daughter was sent away *'beeing with childe'*, probably because the parish in which a bastard was born was legally bound to support it. In the same year the constable was reimbursed two shillings and a penny which he had spent *'convaying criples and other poore people from the towne.'*

Ashby, presumably like other small market towns, attracted some poor people. But larger towns, and especially London, were more attractive. Many of the travellers who were aided by the Overseers were going to London, and doubtless many of the vagrants also went there. In addition, between 1624 and 1638 the Overseers helped at least nine Ashby townsmen, usually young people, to travel to London.

Of course it is not possible to determine whether the period covered by these accounts was normal. The town seems to have prospered during the period immediately before the Civil War. The population was increasing during this period. The average size of inventories between 1621 and 1645 was higher than in previous periods. The correspondence of the traders and bailiffs of the town in later years looked back at the pre-war period as a time of prosperity.

It must also be noted that the first forty years of the seventeenth century are the period when the fifth Earl of Huntingdon lived more or less permanently at Ashby in contrast with the third Earl who had spent much of his time in York as President of the Council of the North. When the family on whom much of the prosperity of the town depended was resident there, and entertained there in 1617 James I and in 1634 Charles I, Ashby was surely more prosperous than it had been in the sixteenth century, or was to be after the Hastings family had left the town.

Ashby, on the eve of the Civil War, may have been, on the whole, prosperous. But about 60% of its population were poor. It must also be emphasised that it was a small market town, in which the wealth of its most prosperous inhabitants was rarely comparable with the wealth of tradesmen in larger towns. Much of this would have been changed by the Civil War.

## II. After the Civil War

Unfortunately there is little direct evidence of the town's social structure after the Civil War.

The Hearth Tax returns are of little use in this context, although they indicate the relative size of towns in the county. In the 1670 returns Ashby contained 216 householders, Loughborough had 413, Melton Mowbray 340 and Lutterworth and Hinckley were almost the same size as Ashby with 225 and 204 respectively. Leicester, of course, dominated the whole county with over twice as many householders as the second largest town, Loughborough.

But these assessments are not reliable as a guide to wealth. In 1663 of the 138 who were taxed in Ashby, 71(51%) had a single hearth, 38 (28%) had two hearths, 11 (8%) had three, sixteen (12%) had four and two people had more than four hearths. John Holland, gentleman, was assessed in 1663 at four hearths, but died within a year leaving goods to the value of only £35. James Orme, innkeeper, who was assessed at three hearths, left only £24 in 1671. Of the four men assessed at two hearths in 1663, and whose inventories were dated within twelve years of the assessment, two left goods valued at between £20 and £30, another left over £150. Peter Byard, cutler, was assessed at one hearth and left, in 1668, £213; two others who were also assessed at a single hearth left over £140 each. In any returns such as the hearth tax assessments, some discrepancy must, of course, be expected between assessment and wealth. Nevertheless all the eight contradictory examples quoted above occurred in a sample of only 28 whose assessments and inventories were known and comparable. According to this sample the average value of the inventories left by men assessed at two hearths (£34) was actually lower than the average for those assessed at a single hearth (£43).

The accounts for the Overseers of the Poor do not survive for this period. But in the years after 1650 a number of new charities were founded.[7] Two of the principal town charities had been established earlier - the Wright charity in 1630 and the Henry Curzon charity in 1633 – but in 1654 Francis Ashe founded a charity which provided weekly lectures in Ashby and exhibitions at Cambridge for boys from Ashby and Derby. In 1661 the Reverend Simeon Ashe founded a charity to give bread and Bibles and to apprentice poor boys. In 1672 James Orme gave land for the provision of free bread for the poor. Elizabeth Wilkins bequeathed money to help the poorest women in the parish in 1697 and Henry Sykes and Richard Hinckley established similar charities in the first decade of the eighteenth century. At least four other charities were founded in the parish in the first quarter of the eighteenth century.

The accounts for the Wright and Curzon charities survive throughout this period, but the fact that between 1657 and 1719 about 250 adults received grants or gowns and 156 children were apprenticed, is not very useful since these charities are not comparable with the poor relief carried out by the Overseers earlier in the century. The Wright and Curzon trustees were under no obligation to help all who needed relief; they simply had to use the funds available to help the neediest.

The inventories from the period after 1645 suggest a general decline in the town. The number of inventories from 1621-1645 is roughly the same as those in the subsequent two periods of 25 years. Yet the average size of inventories before the war was almost £90; in the following twenty five years it was a little over £68; and in the next period a little over £81, despite an inflationary increase over this period of about 5%.

A sample of 23 inventories from the first decades of the seventeenth and eighteenth centuries has been analysed. On average the inventories at the beginning of the seventeenth century included household goods to the value of 33% of total wealth. By the end of the century this had risen to 62%. This suggests that the overall standard of living may have improved during the course of the seventeenth century as more of a person's wealth was spent on domestic, as opposed to agricultural, property.

But this increase may simply reflect the fact that many people had given up farming in order to concentrate on a craft or trade. For example, the two joiners who died in 1707 and 1711 owned virtually nothing apart from their household goods. Both were poor, leaving property to the value of £8 and just under £16. Neither of them owned any livestock.

Of the 25 inventories that have been studied for the early years of the seventeenth century, only three people (one of them a widow), that is 12%, owned no livestock of any kind. Of the 62 inventories from the first quarter of the eighteenth century, 23 people or 37% owned no livestock. Some who did not own livestock were comparatively wealthy but they were ironmongers, apothecaries or innholders.

The inventories do, however, suggest that the first decades of the eighteenth century mark the start of an economic recovery. The average size of inventories for this period was comparable with those for the period before the Civil War. In addition, between 1698 and 1720, a little over 100 people appear to have legally settled in the town. And, as we have seen, a hosiery industry was founded.

Monument in St Helen's Parish Church commemorating Margery Wright, founder of a charity *"to provide gowns yearly for ever, to certain aged and poor people."*[8]
*Courtesy of Chris Jones*

# SIX

# *Agriculture*

I. THE LAY-OUT OF THE FIELDS.

IN 1831 the parish of Ashby is said to have covered 11,200 acres.[1] How far was this area enclosed by 1570? On the outskirts of the parish Alton had clearly been enclosed before its purchase by the Hastings family in the mid-sixteenth century and Ashby Woulds remained an area of common ground until 1800. Blackfordby and Boothorpe were not enclosed to any significant extent before 1570, but little evidence survives as to the lay-out of their open fields.

Professor Hoskins argued that the hamlet of Woodcote had, like Alton, been depopulated and enclosed before 1500, [2] but this is not certain. Woodcote was situated between Ashby and Smisby. In a similar area was a village that by 1570, had been absorbed by Ashby, yet was still known variously as 'Callis', 'Littlethorpe', or 'Netherthorpe'. The name 'Callis' has not been found earlier than a document dated 20 Henry 6,[3] by which time the village of 'Woodcote' has disappeared. On a map dated 1735[4] only 'Calais Town' separated 'Calais Closes' from 'Woodcoate Closes' and 'Woodcoate' furlong. It is possible, therefore, that Woodcote was simply an earlier name for the village known from the fifteenth century as Callis. It is not known if Callis, or Kilwardby, ever had field systems separate from those of Ashby, but by 1570 it is clear that both villages were integrated into Ashby township.

The Enclosure Act passed in 1768 recorded the enclosure in Ashby of the three town fields - the Great Field, the Middle Field and the Lionswell Field - and three commons - the Horse or Brickiln Common, the Goosepen and the Drift (see Map II, page 15).

The Great Field lay to the north of the town, and covered about 350 acres. It may have been divided into two by the Gilwiskaw, and all or part of it was also known as Breach Field. Lionswell Field to the southwest of the town, covered about 250 acres, and was adjacent to Goosepen Common, which was about sixty acres. The Middle Field lay to the west of the town, between Great Field and Lionswell Field, and also covered about 250 acres.

The Horse or Brickiln Common was almost certainly the same area named "Near Common" in the 1735 map since Far and Near Brick-kiln Fields were adjacent to this Common, which covered about 150 acres to the east of the town. The Drift Common was on the west side of the parish and led into Ashby Woulds.[5] The total acreage of town fields was therefore much smaller than the 900 acres in each Wigston field estimated by Professor Hoskins.[6] This may reflect the fact that Ashby inhabitants were not reliant solely on farming.

In 1570 barely a quarter of the parish consisted of the town area; the common fields and the commons. The rest was held directly by the Hastings family as the lord's demesne. By 1735 almost all the lords's demesne – including the 3,000 acres that Lord Hastings had been licensed to impark in 1474 - had been enclosed. Most of this was probably enclosed during the middle years of the seventeenth century and was then divided into separate fields.

It should be noted that most of this demesne probably consisted of areas of marginal utility. This can be seen most clearly in the area known as Southwood, to the north of the town. Not only was this further from the town than any of the cultivated land, but when it was enclosed, the names of its fields indicate the poverty of the soil with five, separate, 'Rough' Closes, a 'Thistley' Close and a 'Stubble' Close. In the 1735 map 150 acres were still shown as woodland. Closer to the town the lord's demesne to the west of the castle consisted of low-lying fields that were probably difficult to drain, known as Pool Flatts; while the hundred acres to the south of the castle consisted of a steep hill, suitable only for rough pasture, on the top of which stood a windmill.

A survey in 1587 suggests that agriculture in Ashby was not flourishing. This survey concluded that, '*The men are (as it appeareth), verie poore and the most p[ar]te of them verie unable to deale for the renewinge of their estates...It seemeth that manie of their tenem[en]ts waxe ruynous and their Land barraigne for want of good husbandrye.*'[7]

But these conclusions may not have been accurate. As the survey was an official one undertaken by the land-lord's agents, the tenants had no incentive to display prosperity. Three of the five surveyors were brothers of the third Earl; another, Roger Bramley, was his legal agent,[8] and only the last, John Norden, seems to have had any expertise in surveying estates.[9] Moreover, only ten leaseholders and eleven copyholders appeared before the surveyors, who themselves admitted that '*the P[er]fecte vewe of euerie p[ar]ticuler mans tenure could not be taken for that the ten[a]nts did not all appear*'. In fact less than one-tenth of the inhabitants of Ashby were represented in the 1587 survey.

The proportions holding land by different tenures in this period were listed by the manorial court in 1574 and 1615.[10] There were 35 - 40 freeholders. A number of these were also listed as cottagers, with rights of common. The 1615 survey listed 29 leaseholders - four of whom were also freeholders - and eighteen tenants at will. There were 206 cottagers, and, of these, 82 had no commoning rights. This gives a total of 266 families which is consistent with a total population of 1,200.

All the evidence suggests that Blackfordby rather than Ashby was the agricultural centre of the parish. In 1627 Ashby contained 40 alehouses, which were most important for a market town, but there were none in Blackfordby a few years previously. The richest Blackfordby men whose inventories survive from the period before the Civil War, held between 65% and 75% of their total assets in livestock, crops or agricultural equipment. None of the Blackfordby inventories give any indication of trade or crafts. Half of the Ashby inventories include references to some trade or craft, although most of them had at least some interest in agriculture. Ashby was, of course, better placed for trading, being upon the roads to main towns.

## II. FARM PRODUCE

It is clear that the agricultural economy of the area was primarily pastoral. Little of the soil was suitable for arable farming, and most of this was enclosed in the three town fields. Most of the bailiffs' letters referred to livestock prices as the most reliable barometer of the town's economy. Special fairs were held for the sale of cattle, sheep and horses. The only mention of a corn market was the rule insisting that all corn must be brought into the open market. Later generations also confirmed that the soil of the parish was unsuitable for arable farming. Monk, when he visited the town in the 1790s stated that *'three parts in four are in pasture'*. [11]

Of the 336 inventories that have survived from the period 1570-1720 only thirty noted individual crops, although a greater number referred less specifically to all or part of their crop as 'corn' or 'grain'. It seems clear that beans were not a popular crop in this part of the county, despite the contemporary saying *'Shake a Leicestershire Yeoman by the Collar, and you shall hear the Beans rattle in his belly'*. [12] Oats and barley were the most important crops in both periods, although wheat was becoming more important in the second half of the seventeenth century. The relative unimportance of wheat in the first half of the century may be illustrated by William Lilly's remark that, when he left his home at Diseworth and walked to London in 1620, he *'saw and eat good white Bread, contrary to our Diet in Leicestershire.'* [13]

Ashby probably practised a traditional crop rotation in its town fields. The earliest reference to three field crop rotation came in the 1337 the *Inquisition post mortem* of William la Souche, lord of the manor, which referred to the 120 acres of land as being worth sixpence an acre, but since only eighty acres were sown each year, this land was worth £2 a year.[14]

In 1710 the manorial court ruled that anyone who had fences between common and fallow, between fallow and peas or between fallow and corn was to repair their fences. This suggests that in this year the Middle Field was fallow, Lionswell Field was the peas field, and corn was grown in Great Field. In Wigston Magna a century earlier one town field was reserved for peas, beans and oats, a second for both winter and spring corn and the third lay fallow.[15]

While there is little evidence about the crops of Ashby, there is considerable evidence about the town's livestock in the surviving inventories.[16] Very few inventories listed no livestock at all, and some of these may have been related to men who had already passed their livestock on to their children. For example, William Joyce's inventory did not include livestock but was valued at £29, of which £25 was in ready money.

But in the period before 1645 almost everyone possessed at least some livestock. Even Edward Jackson of Boothorpe, who died in 1588, leaving £5/10/0 in goods with debts of almost £1/10/0, possessed three cows, a calf and a mare, of a total value of £3/13/4.

45% of the inventories listed pigs. Of the 32 poorest inventories only 4 listed pigs during this period, whereas 19 of these possessed one or more cows, which suggests that poorer men were readier to invest perhaps 20% of their total wealth in a single cow than to buy eight pigs.

60% of the 78 inventories in the period 1621-45 included cattle. The number of cows and calves - 217 of a total of 278 - suggests that Ashby was primarily a rearing centre. The area was not one for fattening cattle, but there may have been some dairying, although the lack of large stocks of cheese suggests that this was not very important.

By the end of the sixteenth century few inventories mentioned oxen and the main working animals were horses.

The numbers of sheep between 1570 and 1595 pose a problem. The average (median) number of sheep included in inventories during these years was 37.5 and the total number was over 1,000. Between 1621 and 1645, when the sample was twice what it had been in the earlier period, the total number of sheep was less than six hundred and the average flock was 14.

The extraordinary number of sheep in the first period was the result of four large flocks. Thurstan Fyldes owned 320, Thomas Baynbrigg, bailiff of Ashby, owned 265, Edward Barnes owned 140 and William Smythe, a tanner, 120. Between 1621 and 1645 only two men owned over 100. Why four large flocks were recorded in the parish in the earlier period is unknown. Possibly sheep recorded in one flock were later sold and recorded again. Certainly when Edward Barnes' widow, Margaret, died in 1612, she no longer owned her husband's flock. When William Smythe died, one of the overseers of his will was Robert Baynbrigg, who was almost certainly the son of Thomas.

In Leicestershire as a whole, the average (median) farm in 1588 included thirty sheep, nine cattle and five horses.[17] Between 1570 and 1645 the average (median) figures for Ashby, excluding the extraordinary figures for sheep in the first 25 years, were between 14 and 20 sheep, 3-5 cattle, and 1-3 horses. But the average number of livestock in Ashby is not representative of the farms of the parish since many of these inventories were of men who were primarily traders. For example, Thomas Casey, a vintner, died in 1614, leaving an estate worth £60/14/8, but possessed only three cattle, one horse and six pigs. An even more striking example is that provided by William Morley, a mercer who died in 1639 leaving almost £350, but who possessed only one 'nag' and a little pig.

It is not possible to estimate accurately the average size of farms run by "full-time" farmers, but three examples of ordinary farms may be sufficient. In 1616 Richard Smith of Boothorpe died, leaving just over £43. Among his possessions were ten cattle, five horses and about 54 sheep. His hay, corn, and agricultural equipment, together with his livestock, were worth 95% of his total inventory. Henry French, also of Boothorpe, was more prosperous. In 1634 his property was valued at £146 and included 25 cattle, 38 sheep, 2 horses, forty pigs and fourteen ducks and hens. His agricultural stock, excluding his bacon flitches, comprised 65% of his total wealth. Finally, Leonard Trenthome was an Ashby labourer who died in 1638 leaving goods valued at £35/15/0. At the time of his death he owned two cows, one mare, six sheep and two pigs. This livestock plus his stock of wood, hay and fern comprised about 45% of his wealth.

The Pains Book[18] has an interesting section suggesting the communal way in which some of the townspeople farmed. *'The herdman shall goe forth of the goosepen with the cattell by sixe of the clocke in ye morning; & not to come againe into ye same penne wth the cattell before vi of the clocke at night'.* Similarly *'ye swineheard shall go forth with ye swine at eight of the clocke in the morning between May day & Michaelmas…and in ye winter at nyne in the morning'* and, like the herdman, not to return before 6 at night. It was agreed that the swineherd would receive 2d a swine each quarter, but no payment for the herdsman is mentioned.

Thus there was one person who was responsible for looking after everyone's pigs during the daytime – and indeed owners were specifically made responsible for ensuring that the swine were kept shut up within their own property before the swineherd took them and after they were returned. It is probable that there was a similar herdsman for the cattle, although it is possible that the first rule quoted above was simply to ensure that all herdsmen removed their cattle out of the Goosepen Common during the daytime. Flocks of sheep were, it seems, the responsibility of the individual who owned them.

# III. Changes in the Agricultural Economy 1640-1720

In the previous chapter reference was made to the agricultural depression in the second half of the seventeenth century. The Earl's stewards complained about the decline in the markets and fairs and there were also references in these letters to agricultural troubles. In 1663 John Davys complained that the cheapness of corn was making the mills unprofitable.[19] Twenty years later Mr. Jacques reported that the frost had locked up the mills *'soe that the Country can hardly get bread or beere'*.[20] Three years later, corn was so cheap that John Swaine, the Ashby miller, claimed that he had lost over £20 in a single year,[21] although nine months later he was ready to take the mills again at a rent reduced by only four pounds.[22] In 1689 Mr. Piddocke recorded that the tenants *'insist upon plowing a piece that for seven years together was plowed, and by that quite beggared.'*[23] In 1690 the price of corn again aroused comment *'Nothing takes any money but Corne and that is att a very lowe rate.'*[24] In 1693 *'Corne and Cattle are att a great Rate yet money is never so scarce.'*[25]

The preoccupation with the price of corn, of course, reflected the stewards' concern for maintaining the rent from the mills.

But the rents of the mills were not the only ones that worried them. In 1670 Mr. Jacques congratulated himself that he had rented out all the land *'and have abated but little rent'*.[26] In 1685 he complained that the collection of rents was becoming increasingly difficult, and in the same year recorded that *'many tennants threaten to leave their grounds at next Lady Day except they have abatements'*.[27] Three years later, in March, he bemoaned the fact that many of the Earl's most considerable tenants had failed to pay anything towards the rent that had been due the previous autumn.[28]

In the same year he tried to comfort the Earl or excuse his own failures, by listing other great lords whose rents were nine months in arrears.[29] In 1689 Mr. Piddocke reported that *'there was a conspiracy amongst divers of ye ten[a]nts about flinging up grounds and getting Abattments, but I hope I have soe managed that, that the back of the plott will be broken'.*[30] Later in 1689 Mr. Piddocke admitted that *'I am forced to threaten some people that I will take from them what Grounds I know they will not part with, to oblige them to keep others.'*[31]

There are a number of rental lists from this period, but they are difficult to compare as the field names rarely recurred in different lists. Nevertheless, the overall pattern of rent changes is clear. In the first half of the century rents tended to rise. For example, Chapmans Close was rented for £11 in 1628 and for £14 in two surveys twenty years later. Aults Close was rented for £2 in 1628 and for £2/10/0 in later rental lists. Far and Near Brickiln fields were rented for a total of £50 in 1628, and for £69 and £70 in later surveys. The rent of Pool Flatt similarly increased from £20 to £28 and £30.

But the 1650s seemed to mark a turning point. Hall Meadow was rented for £19 and £20 in 1650 but for only £16 in 1662 and 1664. The rent of Chapmans Close declined from £14 to £13. The rent of Far and Near Brickiln fields fell from £70 to £64 and that for Hollands Close from £12 to ten guineas. Many rents did not change, but, where they did, most of them fell.

This tendency continued for about thirty years. The 1697 roll, from which the 1681 figures have been taken, provides the only contemporary comparison of rents between two dates. In this survey eighteen rents remained the same between 1681 and 1697, eight rents fell, and none rose.

One further point must be made about the rental changes in the town. As will be seen, the rents of property belonging to the Grammar School rose, while the Earl's rents declined in the second half of the seventeenth century. The school rents, however, had been fixed at the same rate from the end of the sixteenth century until 1683. An official Enquiry in 1657 suggested that they were then one-fifth of what they should be. After 1683 these rents were slowly raised to a sum about one-third of that proposed by the 1657 Enquiry, yet the collectors of the school rents at the end of the seventeenth century still found difficulty in collecting all that was due.

The general agricultural depression was the result of many causes: particularly the economic dislocation of the Civil War; a series of deficient harvests and the cattle murrain of the late 1640s. In Ashby the economic effects of the Civil War were especially important. The overall population seems to have declined at the same time as the community needed to absorb war wounded, such as Richard Cheatle and Eaglesfield.

The biggest change relates to the decline of the Hastings family. The Earl was in 1653 imprisoned as a common debtor, and it appears that the financial difficulties of the Hastings family compelled them to enclose their parkland and sell or lease it on attractive terms. This would account for the eagerness of men to purchase land in the town during a period that was politically unsettled. In the early 1650s this led to 'queues' of would-be purchasers. For example, in 1650 William Chiswell, an Ashby shoemaker, paid £24 to buy the leasehold of a close, a cottage and half a yardland upon the termination of the lease of Thomas Soresby, whose lease was itself only to start upon the termination of the existing lease of Isabell Bucke, the occupier of the property.[32] Similarly, the bailiwick of Ashby was in 1647 held by Thomas Burrowes for life (he was then aged twenty-six), and was then to be held for life by John Greene, and after him by Ferdinand Davis.[33]

Old Park was probably still a park immediately before the Civil War. In 1640, soldiers broke into *'the Earl of Huntingdon's Park at Ashby'* and killed all the white deer, but were unable to catch the other deer *'being more wild'*.[34] Soon after 1660 Old Park consisted of a large number of enclosed fields, and in 1662 nine men were renting parts of this, including, significantly, parts *'not yet measured'*.[35]

There was therefore a land surplus in the 1660s and 1670s, which ensured that rents continued to decline.

The general agricultural depression was reflected in a decline in the number of livestock listed in Ashby inventories after 1646. 66% of the inventories in the fifty years before 1645 included cattle. In the next fifty years this declined to 48%. The corresponding figures for horses show a decline from 52% before 1645 to 33% in the fifty years after 1646. A similar pattern is displayed in the proportions of inventories that included sheep and pigs.

While the numbers owning livestock declined, the average number of livestock increased. This suggests that while many people were ceasing to farm, the larger farmers continued. A reduction in the overall number of farmers brought about an increase in the power of the larger farmers. As we have seen, Mr. Jaques was particularly worried about the *'most considerable'* of the Earl's tenants failing to pay their rents.

Although Ashby remained an open-field township, much of the land surrounding the open fields was enclosed by the 1660s. In 1640 only about one-third of Ashby townspeople were primarily involved in farming and the proportion with no stake in agriculture increased over the following 50 years. But the co-incidence of the trading and agricultural depressions demonstrates the degree of dependence of Ashby traders and the whole community upon the prosperity of the farmers of the area.

# SEVEN

# *Housing*

WHAT sort of houses[1] did these traders, craftsmen and farmers live in? Given the plentiful woodland in this part of Leicestershire, most of the houses were probably timber-framed with wattle and daub filling the panels between the posts. Stone might be used to provide firm foundations for the posts, but would be used above ground level only on high-status buildings like the castle and church. Although there is evidence of sixteenth century brick being used at the castle there is little evidence of such brickwork in domestic houses.

A print dated 1730 suggests the roofs of the houses to the north of the church were tiled, but such houses were in the more prosperous areas of Wood Street and the top of Market Street. The cottages clustered around Ashby Green were more likely to have been thatched. These cottages were very constricted with no land directly attached to the cottage, whereas houses on Market Street used the land lying behind their street frontage to construct outhouses, and pens for pigs and poultry or for orchards or vegetable gardens. Remnants of timber-frames still survive in some buildings in Market Street – for example the Lamb Inn still retains elements of elaborate timber framing internally (see next page).

The inventories for Ashby indicate the numbers of rooms in such houses. Almost all inventories after 1570 which referred to separate rooms mentioned a "chamber", which in this area indicated an upper room above the parlour or hall. The chamber was most often, at the end of the sixteenth century, used for storage. "Parlours" were generally the rooms where the residents slept and the "hall" or

Lamb Inn with detail of internal timber structure dating it to the
early seventeenth century
*Courtesy of Ashby Museum*

"house" was where they lived and, unless there was a separate kitchen, where they cooked.

Two examples may suggest the range of housing in the town. James Collier, who died in 1586, left £11; his house consisted of simply a hall, a parlour and a chamber. Both the latter rooms had beds in them, and the chamber was also used for storing miscellaneous items such as a barrel, a loom, and a tub. The hall seems to have been used both as a cooking and a living area.[2]

On the other hand, the house of Antony Gilby, the Puritan preacher who died two years before Collier, consisted of a hall and parlour, kitchen, buttery and milkhouse, no less than six chambers and a study. It also included, probably separate from the main building, a boulting house and cheese chamber, and a stable chamber, with, presumably, a stable.[3]

Tradesmen and craftsmen must have set aside one room as a shop, presumably next to the street. William Hassard, a shoemaker, probably used his hall as a shop, for there is no mention of a hall or a 'house' in his inventory – just a shop, a parlour and a chamber.[4] William Hatterley, a mercer, had a shop that was separate from his hall, and in addition to these two rooms he had a parlour, kitchen and chamber.[5]

One interesting reference in the Archdeaconry Court, in 1583, recorded that two butchers were prosecuted for *'kepeing theire shopp wyndowes open to sell meats on a Sunday'.*[6] This suggests that the windows were thrown open and the window-ledge thus served as a counter. If this was typical, the shop may have been little more than a shallow space, perhaps shut off from the hall, next to the windows looking out on to Market street. Such a space may have been sufficient for the manufacturer of shoes or gloves; the tailor, butcher or baker, but of course not all craftsmen could have worked in a small space. Nicholas Bowman, a blacksmith who died in 1607, seems to have had a separate building as his shop.[7]

Some alehouses, such as those which were kept only as a subsidiary occupation, were probably just like other houses apart from the fact that the hall was opened at appropriate times to enable neighbours or visiting tradesmen to drink. But a few alehouses were certainly better equipped. Thomas Casey, a vintner who died in 1614, had a house that contained a hall, parlour and five chambers. The parlour was unusual as it was situated on the upper floor, over the tavern. The use of the word 'tavern' suggests that this was not a room used privately by the householder when the alehouse was closed, but was a particular room set aside solely for public use. Casey's house was also the first in Ashby in which it was noted that every room had glass windows. Since this house contained a room known as the 'Scollars Chamber', Casey may have taken into his household one or more boarders from the Grammar School.[8]

The first mention of a glass window in Ashby was in 1580 and glass windows were mentioned in another inventory the following year. It is noteworthy that neither of these inventories concerned the property of particularly rich men. William Taylyer who died in 1580 with a glass window in his parlour left £67, and Hugh Ketle who had two glass windows left only £23.[9] From this period glass windows soon became so common that they ceased to be mentioned in inventories.

Between 1621 and 1645, fifty-five inventories mentioned the rooms in Ashby houses. Some of these may have omitted to mention all the rooms, and a few houses may have been described in more than one inventory, but the sample seems large enough to be compared with a similar list drawn up by Professor Hoskins for Wigston Magna between 1621 and 1642.[10] 22% of the Ashby houses, compared with 37% of the Wigston houses, consisted of three rooms or less. This suggests that Ashby, as a market centre, may have been more prosperous than the almost entirely agricultural Wigston.

Ashby, as a market centre, seems to have been more open to the spread of innovation in the installations of stairs and cellars in Ashby houses. Professor Hoskins noted that no fixed stairs were mentioned in Wigston Magna before 1640.[11] Between 1621 and 1640 three Ashby inventories mentioned a chamber at the 'stairhead' – which suggests a more permanent means of access to the upper floor than the ladder that probably served most houses at this time. Two of these houses were not particularly large. Joan Atkins' house had only two chambers and two parlours.[12] John Tomlinson's house in 1627 consisted of a hall and parlour with three chambers on the upper floor.[13] But Tomlinson's house also contained a cellar. At least seven houses between 1621 and 1645 contained cellars, and one of these had both a beer cellar and a wine cellar. All the cellars, judging by the apparatus that was kept in them were primarily used for storing and manufacturing drink, and most of the cellars belonged to wealthy inhabitants of the town. Cellars were probably an innovation at this time as most references come from the second half of this period.

The enlargement of houses was a sign of an expanding economy. The period of the greatest expansion of Ashby building was probably 1621-1645 since the ten largest houses in this period (each containing eight or more rooms) were all described after 1633. Before 1621 only two inventoried houses contained eight or more rooms.

The paper given to the Earl of Huntingdon in 1638 headed '*A note of all the new errected houses in Ashbye*'[14] has already been referred to in Chapter 3. It is a brief document stating '*in the greene there is twenty and one, at the hill top there is six, beyond the bridge there is three. There is allsoe two smithys. There is two houses in the vickoridge yard. One house in the back lane yt John Byard lives in…Edwarde Hazard's house by ye scoolehouse*' plus three houses which had encroached on either the lord's demesne or the back lane.

The reference to there being 21 houses on Ashby Green suggests that this area is a new development, or possibly the rebuilding of an existing area which had been destroyed through flood or fire. Given that this land is low-lying and prone to flooding, it probably contained

The Bull's Head
This is the oldest house in Ashby according to Scott. There is a tradition that William Bainbrigg stayed here while carrying out his task of making the castle indefensible and uninhabitable after the Civil War. Photograph c1887.
*Courtesy of Ashby Museum*

small cottages for poorer tenants, but the total of 21 houses must have covered more than one side of the Green.

The development of new housing was, of course, of great importance both to the lord and to the town as a whole. Every inhabitant was responsible for scouring the drains, making pavements and shovelling away muck-hills. Unpunished encroachments into the back lane would encourage further encroachments and restrict other residents' right of way.

The type of housing that was being built would also have been important. The risk of fire was very real. In 1604 three houses were burned down, including the house of Richard Spencer, who had fallen out with the Puritan ministers of the town[15]. Throughout the period for which we have accounts for the Churchwardens and Overseers of the Poor there are references to donations to poor people who had suffered losses through fires. In 1687 Humphrey Hollins was fined for burning brass in his yard and *indangeringe the towne'*, and in the same year – perhaps arising from this incident - a penalty of two shillings was ordered to be imposed on anyone who carried '*any fire betwixt house and house uncovered... [or made or caused] to be made in any of their yards any fire or fires.'*[16] In July 1753 a fire destroyed, according to Scott, 150 bays of building or almost one-third of the town.[17]

The Civil War, of course, was a critical point with regard to Ashby's housing. Just a year after the castle's garrison surrendered, a survey was carried out on all '*the Tenements and Leaseholds within the Manor of Ashbye'.*[18] This survey included details of fourteen '*howses pulld downe for which no Rent can bee expected until the same are new built',* including the vicarage and Mr Hildersham's house. The latter seems to have been one of the largest houses in the town. This survey is not likely to reflect the full cost of the damage caused by the lengthy siege of Ashby's castle.

In the years after the Civil War no innovations or enlargement of houses seem to have occurred. In fact, like Wigston,[19] the houses during this period appear to have become smaller, or the larger houses were subdivided. In the later period fewer inventories recorded the names of rooms in which goods were found.

The samples are not large enough to provide firm evidence as to the houses in different parts of the parish. But the 42 Blackfordby and Boothorpe inventories in the whole period suggest that these agricultural villages, like Wigston, may have been slower to adopt new innovations or to enlarge their houses than were the inhabitants of Ashby. No glass windows or cellars were mentioned in any Blackfordby or Boothorpe inventory before 1656, and three of the seven Blackfordby inventories from the pre-Civil War period had no chambers. No Blackfordby houses are known to have exceeded seven rooms between 1570 and 1720.

It seems clear from the inventories that the houses of Ashby reflected the economic expansion of the first half of the century. But, like Wigston, the expansion and improvement of housing seems to have slowed down in Ashby after 1645, reflecting the general economic stagnation of this period.

# EIGHT

## *Law & Order*

### I. THE MAINTENANCE OF LAW & ORDER IN SEVENTEENTH CENTURY

ASHBY was subject to three types of court; the national, the ecclesiastical and the manorial. Evidence is lacking for the first of these three: very few records for Leicestershire Quarter or Petty sessions before 1675 survive. The cases recorded after 1675 suggest that this court was primarily concerned with three types of case: inter-parochial matters, criminal cases, and the licensing of alehouses.

Inter-parochial matters, such as removal and settlement orders and the maintenance of highways were probably of little consequence to most inhabitants of a town except insofar as they determined the size of poor and highway rates. Criminal cases were the most serious, but the least frequent, matters to be decided in the national courts. Between 1675 and 1714 only 3 cases of felonies committed in Ashby appeared at Quarter sessions.

The final matter which concerned the national courts was the licensing of ale-houses. Yet this was not always at the discretion of the J.P.s. As we have seen, when, in 1627, a petition was sent to Quarter sessions in favour of the suppression of some Ashby alehouses, the court refused to act on its own initiative but resolved to *'intreat the assistance of the said ho[noura]ble Earle'* of Huntingdon, *'in respecte of his beinge Lord of the said Towne And of his muche residence there'*.[1]

The ecclesiastical, or Archdeaconry, courts concerned themselves with more immediate issues. They supervised not only matters of church discipline, but also sexual morality and quarrels between individuals; for example, cases involving defamation. These cases will be discussed more fully in chapter ten.

The manorial court was the court whose jurisdiction most affected the daily life of Ashby. The bylaws that were written in a Book of Penal Laws and enforced at this court concerned not only matters of agricultural and trading practice, but also breaches of the peace and maintenance of the highways, Sunday observance, gossip and scandal.[2]

There was some duplication of cases in these three sets of courts. In 1620 the Ashby churchwardens were presented at the ecclesiastical court for failing to present John Gininges and his wife for drunkenness and idle gossip *'who stand presented to my Lord of Huntingdon's court'*.[3] In the 1670s the same four Ashby people who were prosecuted in the Archdeaconry courts for failing to receive Easter communion, were presented at Quarter sessions for recusancy and absence from church.[4]

Over the course of the seventeenth century the balance of power between these courts changed. The pressure for religious toleration weakened the power of the Archdeaconry courts and by the end of the century the number of presentments had declined to such an extent that in most years the churchwardens simply stated *'omnia bene'*. The fact that the Hastings family ceased to reside in the town may have undermined the influence of the manorial court, although the latter continued to function for at least another two hundred years. But since this court had most effect on the daily life of Ashby people in the seventeenth century the manorial court will be the main object of study in this chapter.

## II. THE ORGANISATION OF THE MANORIAL COURTS.

Professor Plucknett wrote that, *'in later times, legal theory attributed to many manors three different courts - court leet, court baron, court customary. But there were practical difficulties in separating the three jurisdictions and during the middle ages there was little attempt to draw fine distinctions'*.[5]

In Ashby the Court Baron appears to have been concerned principally with the transfers of tenancy, and the Court Leet was where the bylaws were enforced. But, in seventeenth century Ashby, these Courts were often combined. They met twice a year; once in spring and once in autumn. As a market town Ashby had separate courts for Fair times, and these, the Courts of Pie Powder, continued to be held until at least the end of the seventeenth century. The manorial courts seem to have been summoned by the bailiff of the manor.

Where did the manorial court meet? In the first half of the century it may have been held at the castle, but there is a tantalising reference in the Book of Penal Laws in 1620 to the making of the pavement from the *'East end of ye Towne Hall'*. In 1682, when the bylaws were revised, the pavement is to be made from *'the East end of the place where the Towne Hall was'*.

It is not clear what happened to the Town Hall – although the Civil War caused a great deal of damage to other properties in the town – nor what the Town Hall was used for. It may simply have been an office, at which the market tolls were collected, or a store for market stalls, but it could have been a meeting place for the manorial court.

The only other reference to the community use of a building is in 1631 when the Overseers of the Poor recorded an agreement between the churchwardens and the overseers with William Astley, pindar, for one bay of his house *'for the town's use'* at the rate of 5 shillings a year. At the same time 13/10 was laid out for the repair of this house but no later payments of this rent are recorded.[6]

By the second half of the seventeenth century the manorial court could not be held in the castle or the Town Hall and on two of the occasions when a meeting place was mentioned - in 1700 and 1706 - the court was held at the Rose and Crown,[7] whose landlord was John Elton. Elton was the bailiff of the market between 1684 and 1689[8] and was in charge of inspecting the weights and measures used by Ashby traders in 1714. In 1696 the court was held in Daniel Wood's inn, The Bell.[9] Daniel Wood held the bailiwick in 1681[10] and it is possible that he and Elton alternated as bailiff, and were accustomed to hold the manorial courts in their own inns. The court was still held in an inn, The Angel, in 1775.[11]

III. THE BYLAWS

The town *'Book of Penal Laws'*, sometimes referred to as *'The Pains Book'*, consists of 182 pages, and contains all the regulations made by the jury of the manorial court between 1620 and 1714.

The 1620 entries were not the first set of rules, and were probably not even the first ones to be written down. In 1638 Robert Newton testified that twenty or thirty years previously he and others forming a jury at a manorial court had forbidden millers from outside Ashby to take corn out of the town to be ground, and he referred to the Pains Book to prove this.[12] No such rule was recorded in the surviving Pains Book.

Forty of the original 90 regulations, and almost half of the 152 new rules brought in between 1620 and 1685 were concerned with agriculture. This concentration of regulations confirms that agriculture in Ashby was still largely a co-operative enterprise: farming open fields and with general rights over commons. Any changes in agricultural practices, unlike those in craft skills, would thus affect everyone.

Most of the agricultural rules were straightforward. Penalties were prescribed for anyone who allowed an animal to stray and graze on another man's land, or destroy his crops, or who allowed a diseased animal to threaten other men's property. Ditches and fences were to be maintained. Swine had to be ringed and the wings of geese to be clipped.

There is one reference in 1620 to a problem that followed enclosure. It was ordered that anyone who had beasts in the middle or far part of Shellbrook Leys *'as it is now devided by p[ar]titions and closes shall have free passage for the driveing and leadeing their cattell both to and from and thorow each those closes there without lett or interrupcon of any soe that they drive them without lingering or leasowing by the waye'.* Shellbrook Leys stood between Goosepen Common and Drift Common.

Social divisions were reflected in these rules through specific restrictions or stints: - for instance a husbandman might keep three old geese and a gander, but a cottager could keep only two old geese and a gander. Protection was afforded to the poorer members of the community. There were separate pastures for cottagers and husbandmen. No husbandman was permitted to put any geese or sheep into the commons called the Cottiers Pastures, and another rule referred to the commons belonging to the husbandmen. Similarly the collection of fern and bracken from the Woulds was controlled. This work was not to start before July 26th; no-one was to employ more than two mowers and men were not to start mowing before sunrise.

Fourteen of the original ninety rules governed traders in the town. As the Earl's mills held a monopoly of grinding the town's corn, everyone was interested in the miller making good meal and taking no more than his due toll. Similarly all the inhabitants of the town were concerned that the bakers baked loaves of full weight, and the Coroners of the Market were instructed to check the weight of all the bakers' produce, and to ensure that it was *'good and wholsom for mens bodies.'*

The Coroners of the Market were also responsible for seeing that no butcher sold any *'swines flesh meazoled or contagious flesh or that died of the murren'*. Butchers were forbidden to *'kill or sell any bull or bulls within this towne except the same be first baited with mastiffs.'* Professor Everitt has suggested that the baiting of bulls was regarded as making the meat more tender, although it would also have provided a free public spectacle.[13]

The alehouse keeper was strictly controlled. Particular town officers were appointed to taste the ale and were ordered to visit every alehouse *'unto every twenty days at the least'* to ensure that full measures were being used, and that the ale was good. In 1700 inspections were changed to once every six months.

As one might expect, given that Ashby was dominated by Puritan ministers at the start of the 17th century, alehouse keepers were ordered to prevent any *'unlawful games'* being played on their premises and for not allowing *'any persons (travailers or strangers excepted) to tiple or drinke in their house above the space of one houre or to staye in their house at prayer time or any other unseasonable times vizt. after 9 of the clocke at night'.*

Two rules were designed to prevent the lord from being defrauded of his full market tolls. First it was ordered *'that noe man suffer any horse or mares to be loaden and to goe down their backsides on the markett day to defraud ye lord's officer of his tole'.* It was later ordered that everyone who brought corn into the town market *'shall bring into the open market all their said corne'* with a penalty for every strike that was *'concealed or set up in any publick or private house during the tyme of the Cornemarkitt'.*

In addition to the rules governing agriculture and trade there were many regulations of a miscellaneous nature. The causeways, bridges, gates and common pound were to be kept repaired and the streets clean. Muckhills were not allowed in the streets and no-one was permitted to winnow there unless he immediately swept up and took away the chaff. Mastiffs were not allowed to roam the streets *'loose and unmoozelled'.*

More general anti-social behaviour was also condemned. *'Any who shall rayle or scold openly ag[ains]t a[ny]of their neighbours to ye p[ro]vokeing or greevyng of them or doing as much as in them lies to take away their credit and good name'* were to forfeit five shillings. Every person who caused an affray that resulted in bloodshed forfeited 6/8, while anyone causing an affray that did not involve bloodshed was to lose 3/4. A fine of ten shillings was to be imposed on anyone who struck or threatened any of the town's officers. The only occasion on which an Ashby officer is known to have been assaulted - in 1695 when John Orton attacked

Robert Ferryman, the thirdborough - the manorial court was unable to deal with the offence, and it was referred to Quarter sessions.[14]

Finally the original bylaws included religious rules. These will be discussed more fully in chapter 10, but it may be noted here that they stand apart from the main body of regulations not merely by their position as the first rules in the book, but also because they are the only class of rules totally omitted in the 1700 revision.

One other change of emphasis in later rules may be noted. Sub-letting and taking in *"inmates"* without permission had always been forbidden. But it appears that towards the end of the seventeenth century there was increasing concern about outsiders taking land, or gaining settlement, in the town. In 1689 it was ordered that no-one was to set his commons *'to no other than the Inhabitants of the Towne'*, and seven years later no-one was allowed to *'sett or let their commons but eat it themselves'*. In 1700 it was stated that no-one was allowed to *'Lodg or harbour any vagabonds cripples wandring beggars or people comonly called Gipseys'*.

During the course of the seventeenth century the status of the ale-house keeper or innkeeper seems to have risen.

This may be illustrated by the career of John Elton. As noted above, Elton was, despite the opposition of Mr. Jaques, appointed as bailiff of Ashby market in 1685, and still enjoyed this position four years later. His inn, the Rose and Crown, was used for meetings of the manorial court, and in 1714 Elton was appointed to inspect the weights and measures used by traders in the town. He was school feoffee from 1689,[15] thirdborough in 1691[16] and organized the Ashby opposition to the grant of a market to Kegworth in 1700.[17] In 1718 he paid the Earl almost £90 a year in rents, which was more than that paid by any other tenant.[18] John Elton was obviously a considerable power within the town, and his career illustrates the commanding position of innkeepers in many urban communities at the end of the seventeenth century.

## IV. THE TOWN OFFICERS

Some of the tasks allotted to the town officers have already been mentioned. No less than six town officers, apart from the lord's officer, or toll collector, had tasks concerned with the market. Two Searchers and Sealers of Leather were responsible for supervising the quality of leather goods. The two aletasters were responsible for checking that the ale was good and its price fair, and the two Coroners of the Market oversaw the market, and in particular checked the butchers' and bakers' produce. They were also stated to be responsible for seeing that the streets were swept, presumably because the weekly markets were likely to have left much litter in the streets.

Four other officers supervised the agricultural welfare of the town. Originally one of the two field reeves seems to have been responsible for ensuring that the bylaws were observed in fields to the east of Ashby and the other in fields to the west, but it is not possible to tell if such a distinction continued. Both field reeves were responsible for seeing that the stints were observed, swine were ringed, fences repaired and levies raised and spent on repairing bridges and gates.

The two pindars had to round up stray animals and shut them in the town pound, and were ordered to present all men who persistently put cattle in fields where they were not allowed. All four agricultural officers were responsible for removing scabbed or infected horses.

The pindars received 2d for every score of sheep that they impounded, 1d a beast, 5d a goose and 5d a pig.

The task of the 'headboroughs', or sometimes 'third-boroughs', is not clear. The outlying areas of the manor — Ravenstone, Blackfordby, and Coleorton - each had one of these officers, who seem to have performed the tasks that the constable performed in Ashby. Perhaps the two Ashby head-boroughs merely served as assistant constables.

The constable was the most senior officer appointed by the manorial court. It was to him that the Lord Lieutenant of the county or his subordinates sent orders, for example, to raise a levy or to exercise the militia, and it was the constable who presented offenders at Quarter sessions. In 1632 the Earl of Huntingdon ordered everyone to be ready *'in the best manner they can in these dangerous tymes to assist'* the constable and his helpers. The exact nature of the danger in 1632 was not recorded.[19]

On a more mundane level, the constable in 1672 was ordered to level and pave the pinfold at the town's expense. But the repayment of officer's expenses was not always prompt. Robert Cantrill, who was Overseer for the Poor in Blackfordby in 1712, had to wait almost 18 months before he was repaid the 25 shillings that he had spent on the village's behalf. [20]

In the Pains Book there is one reference in 1620 to a penalty for anyone who refused to pay *'the Beadle'* his wages. This was repeated in 1686 but no other reference to a Beadle has been found.

The constable was the only official who was formally limited as to the offices he could subsequently hold. A bylaw ordered that no-one who had served as constable might serve in any other office except as churchwarden, Overseer of the Poor, field reeve, or Coroner of the Market. Perhaps the prestige of this office had to be maintained.

The churchwardens had considerable influence. They were responsible not only for the upkeep and repair of the Church, but also for making presentments at the Archdeaconry courts. They could thus maintain a stricter control over the morality of the town than the vicar, who was not obliged to make presentments at the church courts, though often he did.

How were all these town officers chosen? It appears that the manorial officers were elected by the jury at the manorial court once a year. But it is not clear who, in turn, chose the jurymen for the manorial court. The bailiff was charged, in the few documents summoning the court which have survived, with ensuring that a suitable number, usually between 16 and 20, appeared.

The churchwardens seem to have been elected by their fellow-parishioners, although the vicar's influence may have been decisive. In 1666 the vicar of Saddington, Leicestershire, complained to the Archdeaconry court that his two churchwardens had been chosen independently by his parishioners without consulting him.[21] In 1625 the Overseers of the Poor gave 4d to William Astly, partly towards the relief of his sore leg, but also *for summoning neighbours to meet about the choise of churchwardens'*.[22]

The tasks of one group of officers have not yet been mentioned. The Overseers of the Poor and the Overseers of the Highways carried out the functions implied in their titles. The latter officers do not seem to have been particularly active in Ashby. In about 1620 an Overseer of the Highways actually prevented work being started, as a letter in the Hastings collection recorded that *'the whole Towne having made an assessm[en]t for the repayre [of the roads]...there is one Hazzard a cottier whoe is allsoe chosen an Overseerer of the Highewaies, that is a refractory fellowe and doth oppose the whole towne...and goeth about to draw others into his obstinacy'*.[23] A lengthy dispute over the obligations of the inhabitants to pay levies for highway repair apparently prevented any work in the 1690s and two years after this dispute was ended the roads were still *'much out of rep[ai]r'.*[24]

The Overseers of the Poor, as we have seen, were very active. On average, during the 1630s, they dispensed almost a pound a week, in sums not usually exceeding a shilling, to the poor of the town. We do not know if the Overseers of the Poor tended also to be trustees of the other charities, since the surviving accounts for the Ashby Overseers of the Poor end in 1638 and those for the earliest separate charity - that endowed by Margery Wright - only start in 1657.

The Overseers of the Poor and of the Highways were primarily responsible to the Justices of the Peace at the Quarter and Petty sessions and were not mentioned in any specifically manorial documents since they were parish rather than manorial officers. They seem to have been elected in much the same way and perhaps at the same time as the churchwardens.

The number of people who thus served as town officers was large. In any one year thirteen men, and occasionally women, were elected to manorial offices. In addition there were three or four church officers and four Overseers of the Poor and two of the Highways, not counting the self-perpetuating trustees of the school and town charities.

There are few records of men who served as manorial officers in the middle of the century. But an examination of the lists of town officers and jurors 1685 - 1689 and 1705 - 1709 reveals very similar results. First, most of the town officers also served, in different years, as jurymen. In the first period, a total of 71 people were either town officers or members of the manorial jury. Roughly half of the names in each list were repeated in the other, but there were very rarely two members of the same family participating in the administration of the town simultaneously.

This means that, at a time when the population was about 1,200, almost one-third of the families in the town had a member who helped in running the town.

Some officers held a particular office for considerably more than one year. James Lewin was Coroner of the Market from at least 1682 until 1697. Lewin may have been looked upon as an elder statesman of the town, for he was baptised in December 1612 and remained a shoemaker in Ashby until his death in 1699. The Searcher and Sealer of Leather, who presumably needed specialist knowledge, might also remain in office for several years. Richard Cooke, a tanner,[25] was Searcher and Sealer of Leather between 1684 and 1692.

In contrast, no-one in either period held the office of constable, of field reeve, or of headborough for Ashby for more than a single year.

The pindars were different from other town officers because this office seems to have been given to poorer members of the community to help eke out a small income. From 1685 to 1696 the pindars were William Hood and Margaret Braddock alias Purchener. The latter received help in the form of clothes from town charities seven times between 1676 and 1697. After her death in 1698 her role as pindar was taken over by her daughter Mary, who also received a charity gown in 1713. Between 1700 and 1709 Mary Braddock's colleague was Edward Taylor who received help from the same two town charities at least eight times between 1691 and 1719.[26]

With the exception of the pindars, the town offices were held by men of a particular social position. Sixteen men who served as town officers and jurymen have been studied in particular. Of these, seven left inventories, each of which totalled over £50; the father of another left an inventory totalling £213 and the widow of another left £69. David King was clearly a prosperous trader who, in 1667, was prosecuted for issuing his own brass halfpence. A second, Thomas Pratt, was in 1697 renting land from the Earl of Huntingdon at £43-18-0 a year. Others were assessed for hearth tax as having substantial houses (three or more hearths). Only for John Falkingham is there no evidence as to his wealth except that he was honoured with the prefix 'Mr'.

All these men therefore were, at one time in their lives, wealthy, although Anthony Throne seems to have lost most of his property in a fire in 1687.[27]

Ten of these sixteen men were specifically described as traders or craftsmen. Another three were probably traders - Francis Leake, was prosecuted at Quarter sessions for using a false strike,[28] and either John Roby, or his son, was a tanner. Peter Byard's father was a cutler and his son probably continued in his father's trade. The occupations of Thomas Pratt and John Falkingham are unknown. Daniel Wood called himself a husbandman, but as he was described in 1696 as an innkeeper, the term 'husbandman' may not have been an accurate reflection of his primary occupation.

The town officers elected at the manorial court were predominantly, therefore, traders or craftsmen. But they were not necessarily able themselves to write out their lists of presentments for the manorial court. Five of the sixteen appended their names to a petition addressed to the Countess of Huntingdon in about 1671. Two of these five men made marks.[29]

One man may perhaps serve as an example of the type of person who was elected as town officer. Martin Farnell was born in 1634 in a village about four miles from Ashby, and did not take up residence in the town until about 1662, at the age of 28.[30] Ten years later he was elected constable,[31] and two years afterwards was appointed as feoffee of the school,[32] and in that capacity was responsible for the school accounts in 1679 and 1687. He served as churchwarden in 1686, as field reeve in 1685/6 and as a juryman at the manorial court at least four times in the 1680s.[33] He was a baker who, by 1670, had a house containing three hearths,[34] and in a sample of five years' court records - 1682 to 1687 - he was fined for offences against the Assize of Bread at every court. He left the town in 1692 aged 58.[35]

Before we consider the enforcement of rules which Farnell's regular prosecution at the manorial court raises, one other point may be noted. It seems clear from Farnell's career that a man who was respected enough to serve in an office such as constable was also likely to serve in other positions not necessarily concerned with the manor. As another example, Nicholas Sykes, tanner, served as constable and field reeve and, on several occasions, as juryman. He was also at various times a school feoffee, a trustee of all three town charities whose accounts have survived, a churchwarden and a sidesman. Thus a man who served the town as manorial officer, probably served in other offices.

## V. THE EFFECTIVENESS OF THE MANORIAL COURT.

Only two of the bylaws show a clear sectional interest: those concerned with the market tolls were obviously designed to protect the rights of the lord of the manor. Other rules, in particular the rule restricting rich men from employing many mowers to cut all the fern and bracken, seem designed to protect the poor. But were the bylaws enforced in an impartial manner?

First, it is clear that Farnell was not able to use his influence to avoid being prosecuted at court, even in the same years as he was holding manorial and church offices. Similarly, in 1687 Humphrey Hollins who was to be elected town thirdborough the following year, was fined 1/- for burning brass in his yard and *'indangeringe the towne'*. Edward Mason who was a juryman in 1689 was fined 2/- for keeping a fence open, and Nicholas Fowler, field reeve in 1689, was fined for refusing to let the aletaster taste his beer.[36]

Officers were prosecuted if they were negligent in carrying out their duties. In 1690 alone the thirdboroughs of both Coleorton and Ravenstone were fined for failing to present reports; one juryman was fined for failing to appear and both field reeves were fined 3/4 for negligence.[37]

In May 1691 it was felt necessary to order that all officers were to present their accounts within three months of giving up office. In 1705 this was changed to within a single month, and the Overseers of the Poor were ordered to give up their accounts before their successors raised a new levy. Nevertheless at least two of Ashby's constables and also two of the churchwardens failed promptly to surrender their accounts between 1705 and 1714.[38] On eight other occasions between 1682 and 1714 officers were fined for negligence. In 1705 the two Searchers and Sealers of Leather were guilty, although both continued to serve the town in the same capacities for at least four years, without further recorded incident. On four occasions one or both of the field reeves were prosecuted.

That so many officers were prosecuted implies that their negligence was exceptional. Had there been no, or very few, prosecutions for negligence then there would be some grounds for concluding that the officers had established a tradition of indifference to their duties.

Since records of court fines exist only for the period after 1682, it is not possible to compare the corruption or negligence of the officers at different periods. But it is difficult to believe that the manorial court was less effective earlier in the century, when the lord of the manor was resident and able to see that order was maintained. The Puritan ministers also, as we shall see, were very active in prosecuting for offences against church discipline and immorality.

During the seventeenth century the character of the social offences presented at the manorial court changed. Early in the century the bylaws concerning the Sabbath were strictly enforced, but in 1700 these bylaws were omitted. Similarly, absence from church ceased to be a punishable offence after the Toleration Act of 1689.

There was also a decline in the number of prosecutions for immorality, and such prosecutions as there were - for example, the interrogation by Blackfordby chapelwardens of Mary Creswell about her child in 1684 - seem to have been less concerned with making a public example of an immoral woman than to establish who was responsible for supporting the child.[39]

The court records at the end of the century give some indication of the effectiveness of the manorial court at that time, and a clear idea of the type of offences that most frequently led to punishment. Fines for absence from court were among the most frequent penalties that were imposed, but the fine for non-attendance was only 4d.

Apart from non-appearance at court, the greatest number of prosecutions during these years was for trading offences. In a typical session, that for May 1698, 42 butchers were fined for killing calves before they were five weeks old, sixteen bakers had offended against the bread laws, and 20 innkeepers against the ale laws. Thirteen people were prosecuted for various agricultural offences.

The regularity with which trading offences were presented at the court is significant. As we have seen, Martin Farnell was prosecuted at every court whose records survive between 1682 and 1687. He was not the only one. During this 5 year period, the fines for seven sessions survive. Of the 74 butchers fined for killing calves, almost half were fined five or more times. The comparable figures for sellers of ale and of bread are just as striking. Of the 33 bakers, 19 were fined five or more times. The regularity of such prosecutions suggests the manorial court was ceasing to be an effective means of maintaining law and order. The fines of 2d a session were clearly too small to act as a deterrent.

Why was the court continued? First, it was important to the Earl as the basis of his local influence. The Earls seem to have been ready to use the manorial court for their own private purposes. For example, Job Smith was fined at Ashby seven times between 1710 and 1712 for various offences. He might have been a particularly anti-social person. In 1710, however, the Earl of Huntingdon began the second of three law-suits over the boundary between the manors of Seal and Ashby.[40] The manorial lord of Seal was John Alleyne, and one of his tenants was Job Smith, whose property, Gresley Mill, was close to the border between Ashby and Seal. It seems clear that the Earl was using his local influence to prevent, or to avenge, his final defeat in the Queen's courts.

Secondly, although trading offences incurred the largest number of fines, other - less frequent - penalties may have been much more effective. In 1705 two men were fined 6/8 and 13/4 for leaving a horse and mare in a town field. Hugh Copley, in 1709, was fined 6/8 for 'rescuing' sheep from the pindar.[41] Fines such as these were not negligible.

So the manorial court remained significant in respect of certain offences. As long as bylaws were essential, so was the manorial court, and as long as the whole population of the town lay within the jurisdiction of the court its influence was important.

Two changes in the eighteenth century resulted in the court's decline. The enclosure of the town fields and commons in 1768 made most agricultural bylaws irrelevant, and by the end of the eighteenth century perhaps only a third of the town was subject to the court's jurisdiction. At the end of the seventeenth century over 300 people owed suit to the court, which must have been the head of almost every family in the town. In 1775 only 180 were listed on the suit roll even though the population of Ashby by then consisted of about 500 families.[42] So, at a time when the population of the town had increased by about 60%, the number owing suit to the manorial court had declined by 40%. Nevertheless, as late as 1850, Hextall records that Ashby's civil government was in the hands of the Constable and two Headboroughs who were chosen annually at the Court Leet.[43] Even if few people attended this court, the town remained under the control of the officers elected there.

At the end of the seventeenth century the manorial court was still an important social focus for the town, and indeed it may then have been the only occasion on which the whole community - non-churchgoers, Papists and Dissenters as well as orthodox Anglicans - met together in one place.

The town officers remained a self-perpetuating group of fairly wealthy traders and craftsmen. But the number of people involved in the administration of the town was large, and the officers seem to have succeeded in making laws and maintaining order in all but the rarest cases, in such a fashion as not to arouse the resentment of those who were not actively involved in the town's administration.

# NINE

## *Education*

WITH regard to the educational life of the town, the Grammar School, by its success and longevity, can too easily be regarded as the only fountain from which knowledge flowed. Yet by 1720 there were at least two other educational charities operating for the benefit of Ashby children. In addition there were, without doubt, several 'dame' schools which, for a fee, conferred upon their pupils the benefits of at least partial literacy.

In some respects, indeed, these lowly establishments were of greater importance to the people of Ashby than the more prestigious Grammar School. Yet it is the latter which has left more records and, therefore, it is with the Grammar School that this chapter will be first, and more extensively, concerned.

### I. THE FOUNDATION OF THE GRAMMAR SCHOOL.

The date of the formal foundation of Ashby-de-la-Zouch School was August 1567, when eight trustees were entrusted with various properties for the purpose of providing a teacher to instruct *'youths, children and infants in good manners, learning, knowledge and virtue'*.[1] This deed probably confirmed an existing Institution, for it referred to an existing tenement called *'Le Scholehous'*, and a case in the Archdeaconry Court in, probably 1578, referred to old church lands that *'now and hath bene for the space of xvi yeares last past or ther abouts converted and imploied to the maintenance of a scoole within the Towne'*.[2]

The 1567 deed is important because it gave the school a legal existence, and defined the powers and responsibilities of the feoffees. Through this, Ashby school was spared the long legal wranglings which the trustees of the Burton Charity in Loughborough had to endure.[3]

Eight inhabitants of Ashby were appointed as the original feoffees, with the duty of appointing eight further trustees when their number was reduced to six. The feoffees were, as might be expected, all leading townsmen. Anthony Gilby was the Earl's chaplain and Thomas Widdowes the vicar. William Smith was probably the tanner who died in 1576, leaving almost £400 in property,[4] and William Atkins can be identified as the merchant who died in 1602 leaving over £100.[5] Ottwell Hollinshed was described as a 'gentleman' when he was buried in 1568,[6] John Loggan was an innkeeper[7] and Thomas Baynbrigg was the bailiff of Ashby.[8] No information can be found concerning the final feoffee, George Downes. Significantly, Baynbrigg and Smith were also tenants of two of the school properties.

## II. The Grammar School before the Civil War.

The school's *'Statutes and Orders'* dated 1575[9] and, from 1594 onwards, a detailed accounts book,[10] plus the published works of two Ashby schoolmasters and two of their pupils, together with an Enquiry into the school carried out in 1657, give a reasonably clear picture of the history of the school during the seventeenth century and the men who were appointed to run it.

In 1594 the schoolmaster was Robert Fullerton, whose will, dated January 1596/7,[11] gives some indication of the breadth of his interests. He possessed the Puritan books that one would expect from a man of this period but also mathematical books, books on physics and natural philosophy, together with *'Mr. Broughton's map of the world'* and three other maps, as well as French, Latin and Greek books, a Hebrew Concordance and the Pentateuch in Arabic. Robert Fullerton does not seem to have had any great financial need to teach. Despite a school salary of only £14 a year, he owned luxuries such as a *'nutt of India made into a drynking cup with sylver'*, a *'pennerinkhorn of bone with 2 quilted balls'*, a fine wardrobe, an *'angling rod of cane with appurtenances'*, a *'Tobacko pipe with half an ounce of Tobacko'* and a *'purs wrought with silk and silver'* as well as a splendid library.

George Ainsworth was the schoolmaster five years earlier, when the school celebrated three pupils progressing to Emmanuel College, Cambridge. William Bradshaw, born in Market Bosworth, went on to become a well known Puritan divine.[12] Joseph Hall, born in 1574 at Brestop Park in Ashby, was the son of the bailiff, and became a Bishop and a noted supporter of the established church employed by Archbishop Laud to defend *'The Divine Right of the Episcopacy'.*[13] Hugh Chomeley, the third Ashby scholar to enter Emmanuel in 1589, was a close friend of Hall - according to the latter, they were for many years *'partners of one bed'* [14] –who in 1628 was appointed Hall's chaplain at Exeter, and subsequently canon and sub-dean.

This early connection continued between the school and Emmanuel College, Cambridge. In 1654 Francis Ashe left £20 a year to the Ashby school feoffees for the endowment of a weekly lecture, and the property which brought in this sum was placed in the hands of Emmanuel College. At the same time Ashe endowed ten exhibitions at the College, each of ten pounds a year, for pupils from Derby, or from Ashby.[15]

In 1600 the feoffees appointed John Brinsley as schoolmaster at Ashby. William Lilly, the astrologer, was educated there under Brinsley's mastership and has left a vivid account of this in his *'History of His Life and Times'.* Brinsley was *'of great Abilities for instruction of Youth in the Latin and Greek Tongues; he was very severe in his Life and Conuersation; and did breed up many Scholars for the Universities.'*[16]

Brinsley was concerned with the theory of education and in 1612 published a book on this subject, entitled *'Ludus Literarius or The Grammar Schoole'.*[17] This book was *'Intended for the helping of the younger sort of Teachers, and of all Schollers, with all other desirous of learning'.* It aimed to show *'how to proceede from the first entrance into learning, to the highest perfection required in the Grammar Schooles, with ease, certainty and delight'*.

It is perhaps most interesting to compare this book with the original *'Statutes and Orders'* drawn up for Ashby School in 1575.[18] Of this latter we have only a version dated 1715, but this was stated to be, and witnessed as, a *'true Coppy'*.

Both documents decreed that school should start at six with an hour of prayers and a Lecture. The teaching was to start at 7 a.m., although the Statutes allowed a later start in winter. The latter also ordered school to end at 5 p.m. whereas Brinsley advocated 5.30, although this discrepancy may have been the result of Brinsley taking into account the prayers which the Statutes stipulated should be said at the end of the teaching period.

There was also broad agreement between the two on the question of curriculum. The emphasis in both was upon religion. Scholars were to attend all the church services. When there were no services the master was to hold private prayers for the school. Pupils were expected to repeat sermons which they had heard, and thereby develop a retentive memory.

Of academic subjects, the Classics predominated and the higher forms were forbidden the use of English. As soon as Latin and Greek had been mastered to the extent that scholars could compose extempore verses upon any theme, and could hold disputations, for the winners of which Brinsley promised prizes, then, at least in Brinsley's time, the pupils moved on to Hebrew. Lilly noted that Brinsley *'never taught Logick, but often would say it was fit to be learned in the Universities.'*[19]

Both Brinsley and the *Statutes and Orders* emphasized the importance of training the memory. Brinsley stated that there should be exercises for this every day. The Statutes ordered, among other exercises, that every Friday *'the schollers shall repeat and say without book and Construe'* all that they had learned earlier in the week.

101

William Lilly (1602-1681)
*Copyright National Portrait Gallery, London*

Both emphasised the responsibility of the schoolmaster. Brinsley listed four requirements for a schoolmaster, among which he stated that the master should apply himself completely to his work and never absent himself except on an occasion of the most urgent necessity. The Statutes concentrated on listing the tasks which the schoolmaster should not avoid and allowed him only *'one half houre in the forenoon and another in ye afternoon to recreate himself'*.

But Brinsley was extremely doubtful of the efficacy of the monitorial system upon which the *Statutes and Orders* was largely based. Under this system *'praepositors'* were not only appointed to check that all boys avoided speaking in English, a practice of which Brinsley grudgingly approved, but the older boys were to teach the younger ones. *'One of the Schollers of some one of the higher formes'* was each day appointed *'to teach the lowest forme and such as learn to Read, And he shall teach them the eight parts of Speech and every morning hee shall hear them say some part of what they have learned.'*

Ideally, Brinsley advocated a separate school in which reading and writing were taught, but if this was impossible an usher was essential. Although the master should check upon the usher every day, it would be the latter's responsibility to train the younger boys until they were fit to be taught by the master.

Brinsley seems to have succeeded in persuading Ashby feoffees that the single master provided for in the original deed was insufficient. In the school accounts for 1600 the first payment is made to 'Mr. Georg Ward the usher' and within a few years the practice of employing an usher had become regular.

Both Brinsley and the Statutes agreed about the need for, but careful selection of, suitable physical recreation. Brinsley insisted that he would order *'All recreations and sports of Schollars, would be meet for Gentleman. Clownish sports, or perilous, or yet playing for money are no way to be admitted'*. The Statutes decreed that any boy who failed to profit from learning was to be expelled, while Brinsley hoped that learning could be a *'delight both to Masters and Schollars'*. The boys could become *'absolute Grammarians'* and fit for University by the age of fifteen *'without that usual terrour and cruelty, which hath bene practiced in many places'*. Although *'sparing the rod where necessitie requireth is to undoe the children'*, undue anger was to be avoided, and one of the requirements of a good schoolmaster was a *'loving and gentle disposition'*.

His pupil, Lilly, however, remembered little of the delights of school, but recorded *'In the 14th year of my age, by a fellow Scholar of swarth, black complexion, I had like to have my right Eye beaten out as we were at play; the same year, about Michaelmas, I got a Surfeit, and thereupon a Fever, by eating Beech Nuts'*.[20]

Perhaps as a result of the Puritan teaching of his schoolmaster and the Ashby vicar, *'In the 16th Year of my Age I was exceedingly troubled in my Dreams concerning my Salvation and Damnation, and also concerning the Safety and Destruction of the Souls of my Father & Mother; in the Nights I frequently wept, prayed & mourned, for fear my Sins might offend God.'*[21]

Nevertheless, Lilly remarked that *'every of those Scholars who were of my Form and standing, went to Cambridge and proved excellent Divines, only poor I, William Lilly, was not so happy'*.[22]

In the same year as Lilly was *'by reason of my Father's Poverty...enforced to leave School'*,[23] John Brinsley was also forced to resign from the mastership at Ashby, probably as part of a general campaign against Leicestershire Puritans. Brinsley was, in 1615, one of the hundred parishioners who followed their vicar's lead in refusing to take Communion from his successor. But on being prosecuted for the third time, at Easter 1617, Brinsley confirmed that *'he hath a purpose to leave his schoole at Ashby shortely & yett to thend he may gett his Michelmas spipend [sic] desireth to be'* reconciled.[24]

Brinsley's immediate successor was a certain John Watson, who was replaced within a year by Robert Orme, who seems to have found Ashby to his liking and proved acceptable to the feoffees for he continued to hold the office of schoolmaster for the next 27 years.

The size of the Grammar School in this period is unknown, although the fact that, by the mid 1630s, an assistant teacher was required suggests that there were probably not less than forty or fifty pupils. It is also difficult to estimate what section of the population the school was serving at this time for we rarely know the names of pupils at the school except those who were able to proceed to University. The latter were clearly the sons of the wealthier and better educated men of the district. For example, Nathaniel was the son of Anthony Gilby, and Samuel, of Arthur Hildersham. Joseph Hall and Hugh Chomeley were representatives of the same social class.

But the example of Lilly suggests that the school was not simply the resort of the sons of prosperous gentry on their way to University. Lilly was born about 8 miles from Ashby in Diseworth, *'an obscure Town...a Town of great Rudeness, wherein it is not remembred that any of the Farmers thereof did ever educate any of their sons to learning',*[25] apart from the author. He was educated only because of the determination of his mother who intended *'I should be a Scholar from my Infancy, seeing my Father's Backslidings in the world, and no Hopes by plain Husbandry to recruit a decay'd Estate.'* [26] But his father's financial situation forced Lilly to leave school early and in 1620, after his father had been imprisoned in Leicester for debt, Lilly walked to London in search of fame and fortune.

In the fifty years before the Civil War, the accounts suggest that the school was in a fairly healthy financial situation. In 1594 the school funds were able to pay almost £11 *'Towards the reparations of the church and other uses of the town',* and in 1595 £3-8-0 to the constable for his expenses in the town's work.[27] Further amounts of varying sums were paid either to the constable or the churchwardens for the benefit of the town during the next sixteen years, including items for particular purposes; for example, in 1605 and 1606 towards the making of the market cross,[28] and in 1608 for the building of Alton bridge.[29] These grants support the idea that the school properties had, within living memory, been used for general community purposes.

The school feoffees had undertaken one task unconnected with the management of the school, namely the supervision of the 'Day-bell' houses. The rent from these was paid to a person to ring the church bell for 15 minutes at 4 a.m. every day. The traditional explanation of this is that the property was donated by an inhabitant who had lost his way, and desired to commemorate his safe homecoming and guide others by the ringing of this bell. These houses were first mentioned in the school accounts for 1628. The feoffees managed to keep this charity separate from the main school accounts until 1807 when the ringing of the 4 a.m. bell, by then declared to be *useless and annoying*, was discontinued by decree of Chancery and the money transferred to the main school funds.[30]

One reason for the healthy state of the school accounts was that both income and expenditure were frozen at the rates that prevailed in 1594, when the accounts book started. The rents from school property, indeed, were to remain static for almost a hundred years. The schoolmaster's salary, which had not been generous in 1594 at £14 a year, was only increased to £19 in 1632. The Leicester master had received £20 a year since 1574[31] and the Loughborough schoolmaster the same sum since 1615.[32] But the Ashby master's salary was to remain at about £19 until 1683. This salary was probably augmented by taking in boarders, which may help to explain the numbers of non-Ashby boys educated at the school later in the century.

The school finances were also safeguarded because the feoffees seem to have been reluctant to repair the schoolhouse, assuming that was part of the responsibility of being schoolmaster. Between 1594 and 1606 the Accounts Book recorded no expenditure on the repair or equipment of the schoolhouse except the purchase of a school table in 1601. In 1606 an agreement was reached that Mr. Brinsley should have an extra £1 towards the repair of one side of the schoolhouse. And that *'from tyme to tyme hereafter the feoffees shall repair the house, soe farr as the school reacheth; and that Mr. Brinsley himself shall repair it, soe farr as his own dwelling house goeth'.*[33] In 1616 the feoffees allowed Brinsley a further thirty shillings towards the repair of the schoolhouse, but with the proviso that this was *'not as a thing wee held ourselves any way bound unto but as a meer benevolence and gratuity'*. By 1620 the building was in a dilapidated condition and major repairs had to be undertaken.

The site of this schoolhouse is uncertain, although it is traditionally assigned to a position on or near the present vicarage, to the north of the church. The 1620 repairs reveal that the building was tiled, with a brick floor. From 1634, glazing the school windows becomes a frequent item in the school accounts. There is no mention of any expenditure on fuel or for lighting which suggests that the boys may have brought their own, or it may have been provided by the schoolmaster.

It is not possible to discover from the accounts whether the schoolhouse walls were of stone or half timbered. In 1624 6 loads of sand and 5 strikes of lime were delivered to the school, but these may have been for use either as mortar, or as plaster for the walls, or, if there was an upper floor, for spreading over the rushes laid upon the joists to create the flooring.

The feoffees' worries, however, over the cost of repairs were to prove of little consequence. In 1643 an item of one shilling was spent on removing *'the chestes and bookes from the school howse'*. This expense presumably relates to the fact that *'the schoolhouse formerly erected for the use and intent aforesaid in Ashby aforesaid was by the violence of Souldiers pulled downe and raced to the ground and all the materialls thereof converted to warlike imployment'*.[34]

## III. The Grammar School after the Civil War.

The destruction of the schoolhouse did not prevent the Grammar School from continuing to exist in some form in Ashby – perhaps in a private house or the church. The Accounts Book became more confused, in that rents were paid more slowly, but annual accounts continued during the war and the Interregnum until the Enquiry of 1657.

The lack of proper facilities was probably one of the main reasons for the rapid turnover of masters in this period. In 1657 Commissioners were appointed under *'An Act to redresse the misimployment of Lands Goods and Stocks of Money heretofore given to charitable Uses'* to investigate Ashby school. The Enquiry's report gives no indication as to why it was started. Six of the school feoffees, including one who was also a tenant of school property, agreed to act in accordance with the Enquiry's decisions, but the other seven refused even to appear. Three of these, the Commissioners established, were school tenants as well as feoffees.

The Commissioners accordingly appointed new feoffees, none of whom had previously acted in that capacity. The bitterness of the old feoffees was reflected in the Accounts Book where three pages were left blank except for *'The names of those that required us that are ffoeffes to for baer to Act as ffeoffes and that tooke upon them selves to Act for ye schoole: And this blank paper is for them if they please to enter theire accompts'.* The pages remained blank.

As a result of their investigation the Commissioners condemned the old rents as being totally unrealistic and instead proposed new ones up to 10 times higher. Unsurprisingly, the majority of the school tenants opposed the rent increases. Of the five who did not oppose the increases, two faced no increase, and one was one of the new trustees.

But the Enquiry had little immediate effect upon the rents, for Lord Keeper Bridgman refused to order the increases until the leases granted in 1594 had expired.[35] And so in 1660 the old feoffees regained control and the rents remained at their old level. It was not until 1683 that there was any significant increase in the rents. In that year sixteen of the twenty eight tenants agreed to higher rents *'for the next forty years'*, and in that year the master's salary was doubled to a little less than forty pounds.[36]

Old animosities died away. In 1674 new feoffees were elected by the five survivors of the old feoffees, and four of the nine new trustees were men who had been appointed as trustees in 1657.

During the 1657 Enquiry no complaint was made concerning the educational standards of the school. The schoolmaster was considered a fit man, yet without a schoolhouse the school cannot have been large. In 1669, however, the feoffees appointed Samuel Shaw as schoolmaster. Even the manner of his appointment suggests that the feoffees regarded Shaw as something more than a stop-gap, for the agreement between the feoffees and their new master was solemnly enrolled in the Accounts Book.

Samuel Shaw was the son of Thomas Shaw, a blacksmith at Repton. In 1656 he was appointed master at Tamworth Grammar School. He was ordained minister by the classical presbytery at Wirksworth in Derbyshire and subsequently presented to the rectory of Long Whatton in Leicestershire. From this he was ejected in 1661.

The details of Shaw's early life were recorded by his biographer, Edmund Calamy, who continued by describing, in some detail, the work Shaw did at Ashby.[37] Calamy was not impartial as the avowed intention of his work was to show the sufferings of those men ejected by the restored Royalists. But there is little reason to doubt the accuracy of Calamy's statement that on Shaw's arrival *The Revenue was then but small and the School-buildings (those few there were) quite out of Repair, and the Number of Scholars few'. 'And by his interest among Gentlemen, he begg'd Money for the building of a good School, a School-house, and a Gallery for the Convenience of the Scholars in the Church.'* [38]

This statement is confirmed by the dedication of one of Shaw's plays to Sir John Shaw, Baronet, Sir John More, Knight, and Christopher Pack, Esq., *The Principal Erectors of those Walls, wherein it [the play] was contriv'd; as a Monument of Their Beneficence, and my own Gratitude'.*

The school accounts do not show when the new building was completed, as the new schoolhouse was erected without the use of school funds. The site of the new school was upon ground now occupied by the headmaster's house, to the east of the church.

Calamy noted that Shaw overcame the problem of the lack of scholars. For *'His Piety, Learning, and Temper soon rais'd the Reputation of his School, and the number of his Scholars above any in those Parts; so that he always kept one, and for a great while Two Ushers to assist him; having often 160 Boys or more under his Charge. His House and the Town was continually full of Boarders from London, and other distant Parts of the Kingdom, which was a great Advantage to all the trading part'.*[39]

The reference to two ushers to assist him cannot be confirmed from the school accounts as no salary was paid to any usher during this time. Shaw could not have managed what was certainly a large school, even if the number of 160 may have been an exaggeration, without some help. Probably the usher's salary was paid by the schoolmaster, in which case Shaw literally *'kept'* his ushers.

Under Shaw, Ashby school achieved considerable academic distinction. Dr. Fox has listed the careers of twenty two Ashby scholars who entered Cambridge University while Shaw was master. But it must be noted that almost all of these men were born outside Ashby. The only one of these twenty two scholars who was certainly born in the town was Shaw's own son. This list tends to confirm Calamy's assertion that the number of boarders increased considerably.

The difference between this period and the early part of the century is striking. Half of the 22 scholars from Shaw's period were born more than ten miles from Ashby. Eight out of nine pupils similarly

Samuel Shaw (1635-1696)
*Copyright National Portrait Gallery, London*

listed for the earlier period were born within five miles of the town. This might, of course, be the result of very small samples, but it does serve to reinforce the idea that Ashby was becoming a county, rather than a local, school.

Ashby school also gained wider fame because of the publications of its master. Shaw's works included not only theological books, as befitted a prominent Dissenter, and Latin text-books as befitted a schoolmaster, but also three comedies. These plays are of interest for they were all designed for the general entertainment and edification of the school, and were performed by the pupils. Shaw explained his purpose more fully in the preface to his first two plays: *'Words made Visible, or Grammar and Rhetorick Accommodated to the Lives and Manners of Men'.* These plays *'were composed for private diversion and Acted by the Lads of a Country School, where they received a general applause from Just hands and Judicious heads, and certainly since those representations are intended only to modulate the Tone of voice in youth and bring them to a convenient assurance and apt gesture, such subjects...may be as proper and far more useful than* [more conventional plays]. *Schoolboys cannot but be hugely pleas'd to see those Eight crabbed Tyrants, that have so oft occasion'd their smart, now brought to the Bar and contributing to their diversion: to find Rhetorick that was their Toil become their pastime'.*

One of his plays was intended to warn the audience against the dangers of extremism, and included a few interesting pieces of social comment. One character has an outburst against idle gentlemen, before concluding that *'We have a Pious Clergy (especially about Christmas time)'.* Another expressed distrust of *'a Physician, whom I take to be the worst of Diseases...I should ill be content to die, as I know I must, if I cannot be content to be sick'.*

Shaw does not seem to have been a conventional schoolmaster. He believed, like Brinsley, that the best teaching made learning a pleasure. Calamy wrote that *'he was of a peaceable disposition, and was frequently employ'd in reconciling differences.'* It was typical of the man that, although he licensed his school in 1689 for a Dissenters' Meeting-house, he preached there at noon, between the two Anglican services which he, his family, and scholars always attended. Samuel Shaw died in January 1694/5.[40]

The period following his mastership appears to have been uneventful. There were no attempts to change the curriculum, or to adapt the school's facilities to new circumstances. Essentially Ashby school, like that at Leicester, seems to have provided a higher education for the higher social classes, with a curriculum designed to equip pupils for the Universities. It is not, then, surprising, especially with the growth in the number of boarders under Mr. Shaw, that local people became more interested in founding new schools to serve the local population rather than in increasing the endowment of the existing establishment.

## IV. OTHER SCHOOLS IN ASHBY IN THE SEVENTEENTH CENTURY

Evidence about the other educational establishments in Ashby is more fragmentary.

The foundation about which we know most is that provided for by the will, dated 1695, of William Langley, an Ashby yeoman.[41] According to this, land in Diseworth - about 8 miles from Ashby - was to be sold, and the proceeds devoted to *'the teaching and instructing in the Reading of English Twelve poore Boyes or girls'* from Ashby and six from Diseworth at *'some schoole in Diseworth afores[ai]d or in default of a Schoole in some other Towne thereunto adjacent.'*

The pupils were to be taught there for three years only and the master was to receive 1½d for each child every week. Sixpence a year was to be allowed each child during the three years for books *'to learne in'*. An additional 2d was to be given each child for a catechism, 12d for a copy of *'Mr Allens Allarme to the unconverted or some such other good Booke'* and three shillings each for a Bible. Edward Harris of Ashby, shoemaker, John Savage of Ashby, yeoman, and Henry Presbury of Packington were to act as the first trustees and were to be given 10/- each every year *'In Incoragement'* to them *'to bee carefull in executing the Truste afores[ai]d'*.

Langley himself was probably connected with an Independent or Congregational meeting, for he also left £3 towards the repair of an Ashby Meeting-house. *'Mr Allens Allarme to the unconverted'* [42] was a popular non-conformist book, with a preface by the well-known Dissenter, Richard Baxter.

It is interesting that this foundation provided that girls as well as boys should be educated; the pupils were specifically to be *'poore'*, and money was explicitly provided to cover the books the children would need. Langley specified three years for the schooling, presumably, to maximise the number who could profit from this education, while giving the slower learners sufficient time to attain enough literacy to read the Bible or catechism. This was essentially a reading school, since writing and arithmetic, in accordance with the founder's wishes, were excluded from the curriculum for at least a century and a half. The poor were thus provided with only the most elementary education, lest, presumably, they might be educated above their station in life.

This foundation, however, did not achieve all its benefactor's aims. Indeed Langley himself was not certain whether he had left enough money to fulfil all his intentions. At the end of his will he ordered that if the money was insufficient either the legacies to his friends or the number of pupils should be reduced.

In 1838 the Charity Commissioners reported on the Langley bequest.[43] First, the trustees had failed to follow the directions of the will in that they had not sold the land in Diseworth, but had simply leased it every eight or ten years, until 1812. Of the eighteen pounds income in 1838, seven pounds was given to *'the Mistress of Ashby School, for teaching 18 girls of that parish'* and £3-10-0 for the education of nine

Diseworth boys and girls. Five pounds was spent on books and ten shillings given to the trustees. But the separate school that Langley had wanted had not materialised.

One new school, known as the Blue Coat School, was successfully founded in the town during this period. The exact date of this foundation is unclear. Nichols stated that it was established, primarily by Isaac Dawson, *'in or after 1669'*.[44] The Charity Commissioners, however, reported that it was founded by the transfer of land worth £45 to John and Leonard Piddocke in 1719.[45]

Nichols' lively account of the foundation related how Isaac Dawson, an Ashby apprentice, was sent by his master to Lincolnshire. On this journey he was robbed by three highwaymen, but later recognised his horse at an inn. The consequent capture of the highwaymen brought Dawson a £40 reward, which he then gave towards the foundation of a charity school. The first reference to any *'Isaac Dawson'* in Ashby documents is the baptism of Isaac Dawson, son of John, on June 2nd 1694. If this was the man who was the apprentice sent to Lincolnshire, then the Commissioners' dating of the foundation of the school may have been more accurate than Nichols'. It may also be noted that John Dawson, who died in 1716, was fairly wealthy[46] and his son, therefore, would have had no pressing financial need to keep a reward.

Whatever the exact foundation date, by early in the eighteenth century the Blue Coat School was providing instruction for 26 boys in reading, writing and arithmetic, and had a separate fund to supply each pupil with a blue coat, hat and breeches. This charity continued to be supported by townspeople on a voluntary basis. In 1764 it was decided that sufficient funds were available for the school to continue without further subscriptions, but until that date it seems to have survived only because of local people's generosity. This demonstrates the need that was felt, and which the Grammar School did not satisfy, for free, elementary education in the town.

In addition to these charity schools private schooling continued during the seventeenth century. The quality of such schooling must have varied considerably, and such schools survived only as long as the master or mistress found it worthwhile.

Some private teachers taught during a hiatus in their own career. John Bainbridge, son of Robert Baynbrigg, bailiff of Ashby, was educated at Ashby school and Cambridge.[47] Subsequently he returned to Ashby for a short time, maintaining a school while practising medicine in the town. In 1618 he moved to London and subsequently became the first Oxford Professor of Astronomy.[48] Henry Clarke, who was paid by the Overseers of the Poor for *'Beardsley's schooling'* in 1634, was subsequently appointed an assistant at the Grammar School.

Other schools were probably started by men who had been unable to proceed to, or continue at, University, but clung to the privilege which a little learning had given them. Thus William Lilly, after he had been forced to leave Ashby school, went *'to my Father's House, where I lived in much Penury for one Year, and taught School for one Quarter of a Year, until God's Providence provided better for me'.*[49] Such teachers may have helped boys who could not keep up with, or had missed, work at the Grammar School. In 1635 William Brookes was paid 2/6 by the Overseers of the Poor *'for scooleing of a boy of Boultons which was behinde'.*[50]

But most of the private schools were probably kept by widows or spinsters attempting to eke out their income by imparting smatterings of knowledge to the children of parents who were too poor to give their offspring a better education. Thus the Overseers of the Poor between 1626 and 1629 paid Elizabeth Harding, described as 'wife' in 1626, and thereafter as 'widow', 12d a quarter for the schooling of Mr. Thomas Perrins' boy. Nothing further is certainly known about widow Harding, except that in 1625 the Overseers gave her 8d towards the burial of her child.

One private school whose mistress certainly had an unsavoury reputation was that run by Mary Alcocke. The only reference to this school occurs in a case in the Archdeaconry court in 1704 between Mary Alcocke and William Armeston, a tanner.[51] One of the witnesses to this case was Robert Raylet of Ashby, aged fifteen, who went to the Alcocke house *'to read a chapter'*, because Mary Alcocke kept a *'reading schoole'*. Another witness James Bodell, aged 19, boarded at her house. It is not clear if she also taught him reading, but his age suggests that she did not. Bodell was so lame *'yt he cannot worke for his livinge'*, and was therefore maintained by the parish. Lawrence Farmer, an Ashby gentleman, stated in evidence that Mary Alcocke was *'a very Quarrelsome and contentious woman and often at variance with her Neighbours and is a woman of a very bad reputation'*. A shoemaker, William Fleming, described her as *'A Scandall to her Neighbourhood'* and Elizabeth Cheatle stated that she *'hath abused or fallen out with most of her Neighbours'*. No witnesses were called to deny this reputation.

Until the Marriage Act of 1754, which required signatures in marriage registers, it is not possible to assess accurately the level of literacy in Ashby. But it seems clear that throughout the seventeenth century the sons of vicars and schoolmasters - children of the educated classes, in fact - and of the local gentry were well served by the Grammar school. The sons of tradesmen and yeomen may have been satisfactorily educated, at least in the lower forms, for the first century of the school's existence. But as the school's academic distinction increased, more boys were attracted from a wider area. Consequently the Grammar School probably ceased to provide an elementary education for local boys, and, to satisfy that need, new charitable schools were founded at the end of the period.

# TEN

# *Religion*

**B**EN Jonson, in *'The Magnetick Lady'*, printed in 1641, pictured one type of parish priest and the influence that he had upon his flock: *'He is the prelate of the parish here; And governs all the dames; appoints the cheer; Writes down the bills of fare; pricks all the guests; Makes all the matches and the marriage feasts ....draws all the parish wills... Comforts the widow, and the fatherless, In funeral sack'.*[1]

The Ashby ministers in the second half of the seventeenth century may have conformed more or less to this pattern, but from the 1560s to the 1630s, the town was distinguished by the presence in it of several Puritans of more than local importance.

All these men owed their position in the town to the third Earl of Huntingdon, whose *'zealous care to promote the Gospel of Christ'*[2] led him to refound the Leicester Free School, at the same time as he gave a legal foundation to Ashby School, on strictly Puritan principles. The Earl owned at least eight advowsons in Leicestershire and consistently chose to fill vacancies with convinced and often radical Protestants. Dr. Cross noted that some historians have tried to trace the origins of Leicestershire nonconformity back to Wycliffe's incumbency at Lutterworth, but concluded that *'the little town of Ashby-de-la-Zouch seems a much less disputable source for the spreading of radical Protestantism in the county'.*[3]

Henry Hastings, 3rd Earl of Huntingdon (c1535-1595)
*Copyright National Portrait Gallery, London*

# I. The Puritan Ministers; 'A light to all the countrey'.[4]

The most influential Puritan who was encouraged by the Earl to settle in the county was Anthony Gilby who established himself at Ashby.

There is no evidence that Gilby was vicar of Ashby. In 1576 he was described in the *Liber Cleri* as preacher, and *'John'* Widdowes was vicar.[5] *'John'* was probably an error. Thomas Widdowes was inducted as vicar in 1569[6] and died there in 1593.[7] Gilby may possibly have been vicar before 1569, but there is no direct evidence that he was ever more than a 'preacher' there.

Gilby however must have had some connection with Leicestershire before the accession of Queen Mary, for, after escaping abroad with his wife and children in 1553 or 1554, he wrote an *'Epistle of a Banished Man out of Leicestershire, sometimes one of the Preachers of God's Word there'.*[8] In 1555 he travelled to Geneva where he became a *'dear disciple'* of Calvin, and helped Coverdale with the translation of the Bible which appeared in 1560. In 1558 Gilby was one of the reformers who signed a circular letter from Geneva to all other exiled churches for reconciliation. At some time early in the 1560s he took up residence in Ashby.

Patrick Collinson stated that *'Gilby could probably have been a bishop had he so chosen'* [9] and in fact Gilby behaved very much as if he was one. John Aylmer, later Bishop of London, reflected this when he warned the Archbishop of Canterbury in 1576, *'There is of late a rank of Rangers and posting Apostles yt go from Shire to Shire, from Exercise to Exercise...to Ashby where Gilby is Bishop'.*[10]

Gilby's influence is reflected in his correspondence. When, in 1565 he complained to the Bishop of Coventry and Lichfield about the quality of the ministers in his diocese, the Bishop humbly promised to do his best to rectify the situation. In particular he undertook to displace that *'p[er]son of Stretton'* as soon as possible, and *'If the matter will not passe thorowe at Lichfield, I will then sende you worde, and use your counsell'.*[11]

But Gilby himself was also harassed by the Church authorities. In 1571 Archbishop Parker commanded Grindal, Archbishop of York, to prosecute Gilby. Grindal refused, ostensibly on the grounds that Ashby was outside his province, but probably because he feared to displease Gilby's patron, the third Earl of Huntingdon.[12]

About five years later Bishop Cooper, at the instigation of the Queen, suppressed *'Prophesyings'* throughout the diocese of Lincoln. Gilby and his colleagues, however, did not allow the Ashby exercise to be suppressed without a strong protest. Apart from the order in 1575 that the whole of Ashby school was to attend the local *'Divinity Exercise called Prophecying',*[13] this protest at its suppression is the only evidence that we have as to its existence in the town. The Exercise was started before 1570 with the permission of *'them that were in office.'*[14] It had apparently started with a meeting of local ministers who had left the church doors open while they talked and prayed, and other men had come to listen *'and to learne some good lessons in gods schoolehouse'.*[15]

Subsequently the exercises of *'interpreting the scriptures, of fasting and prayeing'* had been continued for the *'edification of the people and to the great conforts of many good consciences that could have no teaching in the Townes wheare they dwelt.'* The importance of a central assembly in a rural area - in *'theise blynde corners about us'* - was emphasised. *'All men do know by experience, that sticks of fyre scattered, can give no suche pearcing heate, as when they are Laid togeather.'*[16]

Apart from the Ashby Prophesyings we know little of how Gilby acted during his stay in Ashby, but, from his correspondence, it is clear that he was a figure revered in the Puritan movement both by former colleagues in exile such as Thomas Wood and Thomas Bentham, and also by the younger leaders such as John Field. Gilby's national influence is confirmed by the way in which he was condemned by supporters of the established Church, such as Aylmer.

Gilby died in 1585. He was survived by the vicar of Ashby, Thomas Widdowes, who had in 1570 married Gilby's daughter Ester.

Whereas Gilby was a leader of national importance, Widdowes was the local leader of a Puritan group of ministers. Henry Presbury, for example, was vicar of Packington from 1558 to 1594. His relationship with Widdowes is clear. He reported, probably in 1570, that a secret marriage had been held in his parish one Wednesday, *'I being at Ashbye at a sermonde as I was Accostomed to be and partly to learne counsayle of Mr Wydowes'*.[17] The vicar's example was followed by his parishioners. In 1576 the Packington churchwardens described how they *'have fownd div[er]s absentt from com[mon] prayer uppon sondayes & holydayes & have gone to seeke them & have lerned yt they wer at Asheby'*.[18]

Local Puritans probably felt a special need for close contact with each other, for Ashby was at the centre of a predominantly Catholic area, an area of scattered villages dominated by the old seignorial bonds. There is little reason to doubt that had Ashby's lord not been a devout Puritan, the town could have become a centre of Catholic recusancy, like Kegworth, only ten miles away. All the Puritan centres in this part of Leicestershire were places where the Earls of Huntingdon were patrons.[19]

Thomas Widdowes, vicar of Ashby, was buried in Ashby in 1593. The third Earl wrote to the man that he had chosen to succeed Widdowes, Arthur Hildersham: *'Since that it hath pleased the Lord to call Thomas Wydowes to his mercy, who was (in my opinion) both faithful, careful and diligent in his function according to his talent, I do wish with all my heart the supply of that place to be such as that which good Father Gilby and he...have planted in and about Ashby may be continued and increased'*.[20] As vicar and preacher, Hildersham was to exert an unprecedented influence in the parish over the succeeding forty years.

Hildersham's parents were both devout Roman Catholics and one of his uncles was Cardinal Pole. His parents intended that he should become a priest, but the young Hildersham was converted to Protestantism by his school master in Saffron Walden. In 1578 he evaded the attempt of his father to send him to Rome, and was introduced to the Earl of Huntingdon. With the Earl's help, which was prompted, no doubt, by the ties of kinship (the Earl was second cousin to Hildersham's mother) as well as the desire to promote Puritanism, Hildersham remained at Cambridge as a Divinity reader at Trinity Hall.

In September 1587 Hildersham settled in Ashby, initially as lecturer. At this time Hildersham had neither been ordained, nor had he a licence to preach. He was consequently forced to a public admission of his faults and in June 1588 was suspended. In January 1592, after he had apparently taken orders, he was allowed to preach north of the Trent, and later this geographical limitation was removed, apparently by the Queen, who recognised Hildersham at court as *'Cousin'*. On the 5th July 1593 he was instituted vicar of Ashby, in succession to Thomas Widdowes.

The silencing of Hildersham between 1588 and 1592 was not the last such suspension. Altogether he was silenced four times during his career, and served Ashby as vicar and preacher for just 21 years out of the 38 and a half years between his induction as vicar and his death in 1632. These suspensions were a result of his position as the leading member of a group which refused to accept the rulings of the Church Establishment as to Church vestments.

Hildersham was not a schismatic but he did not choose themes to please his audiences. When, in 1596, he preached the Assize sermon at Leicester, his views were so unpalatable that the staunchly orthodox Lord Chief Justice of the Common Pleas, Sir Edmund Anderson, rose to leave the church. Hildersham publicly ordered him to stay, and a Grand Jury which was later ordered by Anderson to indict Hildersham, refused to do so.[21]

More famously, Hildersham was involved with the Puritan Millenary petition, presented at Hampton Court in 1604. Hildersham was one of the six principal organizers of the petition, by which the Puritans hoped to show King James the strength of their party in the

Arthur Hildersham (1563-1632)
*Copyright National Portrait Gallery, London*

country.[22] Apart from this occasion Hildersham remained primarily a local leader.

One notable protégé of Hildersham, although he was never a minister within the immediate locality, was Simeon Ashe. Ashe was educated at Emmanuel College, Cambridge, and was encouraged to join the ministry by Hildersham. He later became chaplain to the Earl of Manchester, and an opponent of Cromwell, to the extent that, after the latter's death, Ashe was one of the divines who went to Breda to express support for the restoration of the monarchy.[23]

No biographer has mentioned Ashe's birthplace, but it is possible that this was Ashby. 'Ashe' or 'Ash' was a common name in the town, and, as we have seen, Emmanuel College was a frequent resort of Ashby scholars. An Ashby connection would explain both Hildersham's early influence and two gifts to the town. The school accounts for 1656 list the sum of 3/8 *for makeing up the price, of a dictionary given by Mr Simeon Ashe to the school.*[24] In December 1661 a charity was established by Simeon Ashe to provide ten pounds a year for the apprenticing of two Ashby children and to provide bread and Bibles for the poor of the parish.[25]

The influence of the third Earl was presumably why Gilby, who was more outspoken in his opposition to bishops than Hildersham, was never seriously threatened after 1558, while Hildersham, who was inducted at Ashby just two years before Earl's death, was four times suspended. The fourth and fifth Earls showed little sympathy for Puritan views.

Hildersham was suceeded as vicar of Ashby at, or before, Easter 1615 by William Hacket, who accused his predecessor of being a schismatic, primarily because he refused to receive communion kneeling. Hildersham was persuaded to go into hiding. In his absence he was sentenced to be imprisoned, degraded and to pay a £2,000 fine.[26]

During 1617 three clerics moved, or were moved, away from close contact with Ashby. John Brinsley, Hildersham's curate and Grammar School master, left the town, *'being enforced from keeping school, being persecuted by the bishop's officers.'*[27] Richard Neile, Bishop of Coventry and Lichfield and Hildersham's chief enemy, was translated to Durham, and in the same year Hacket was replaced as vicar of Ashby by Thomas Pestell.

Hildersham was at last re-licensed in 1625 and in September of that year he began his great series of sermons, *CLII Lectures upon Psalm LI*, which were posthumously published in 1635. Despite being suspended for sixteen months between delivering the 143rd and 144th of these lectures Hildersham completed the series. His last sermon was preached on 27 December 1631 and he died on 4 March 1631/2, aged 69.

The death of Arthur Hildersham marks the end of seventy years in which Ashby had been served by a succession of well known Puritans. Forty years in which ministers of national importance had been protected by the third Earl of Huntingdon, followed by thirty years of almost continuous breaches between the ministers and the church authorities must have had considerable impact upon their parishioners.

## II. THE PURITAN MINISTERS: THEIR IMPACT.

The most dramatic display of the influence of the Puritan ministers was described by Chalmers as *'an unmatched spectacle in the sheer volume of nonconformity, expressing active sympathy for their former minister.'*[28] The former minister was Hildersham and the occasion was his third suspension. In 1615 about one hundred parishioners followed Mr. Hildersham and his wife, in refusing to take communion from his successor.[29] The exact number is difficult to establish. John Ashe and his wife appear to have been listed twice, and some people had excuses other than their sympathy for Hildersham. Against the name of

Elizabeth Newton, for example, it was noted *'she is blind & unable to come to the Church'*. Against Margerie Burrowes was written *'apud London'*. But the number certainly included the sidesman for that year, and one of the two churchwardens. The fact that the church officers who had been elected after Hildersham's suspension were sympathetic to his cause, suggests that the congregation possessed more influence than the incumbent, Hacket, in the selection of these officers.

A comparison of the 1615 figures with those for 1612 is striking.[30] In 1612, before Hildersham was suspended, only three inhabitants of the town were prosecuted for *'seldom coming to Church'*, and three others for leaving church before the end of the service.

The demonstration of 1615 was not an isolated event. In 1616 sixty-three parishioners[31] refused to receive communion, and in the following year 58 refused.[32] In 1619 sixteen Ashby people were excommunicated and were still excommunicated two years later.[33]

Refusing to take communion was not the only way of demonstrating Puritan orthodoxy at this time. John Armston was prosecuted in 1616 for *'causing his child to be christned at blougherbie [*i.e. Blackfordby*]...by Mr Hanley minister of Mesam...being an unconformed minister in a bason and not using the signe of the Crosse and for that his wife did not after her said deliuerie yeald thanksgiving in such sort as by law is required'*.[34]

In the same year John Bentley had his child christened at Ashby *'by a strange minister without the signe of the crosse in a bason.....procuring Mr Hackett minister there to be absent'*.[35]

Ashby's proximity to the county, and diocesan, border encouraged some Puritans to take advantage of neighbouring parishes. Calke, where in 1619 Richard and Anne Cotterell were secretly married,[36] was less than four miles away but was outside Lincoln diocese. John Burrowes deposed on behalf of his wife in 1620 *'that his wife hath rec[eived] ye com[munion] sev[er] all tymes within this yeare & halfe but not att her p[ar]ishe Churche of Ashby'*.[37]

Puritanism had a far-reaching effect upon the town in the sphere of education. The foundation of the Grammar School was a result of the Protestant abolition of chantries, and the 1575 Statutes clearly reflected the Puritan beliefs of the third Earl of Huntingdon. Of the eight original school feoffees, two were Gilby and Thomas Widdowes. By 1606 Hildersham was a feoffee.[38]

Of the schoolmasters appointed by these feoffees, most were supporters of the Puritan movement. The appointment of Samuel Shaw in 1669 suggests that the non-conformist influence within the school continued after Hildersham's death. Shaw was one of the ministers ejected from his living by the Act of Uniformity. He later became a leading Dissenter in Ashby, and in 1689 licensed the schoolhouse as a Dissenters' meeting place.[39] But he only preached between church hours and continued to attend the parish church with his scholars.

The example of Shaw, like Hildersham, shows that those who disagreed with elements of the established Church did not necessarily cease to be communicating Anglicans. In the Compton Census of 1676 the vicar was able to list 672 communicants, one Papist and only five Dissenters.

Lilly asserted that the Puritan tradition persisted during the war; *'most of the People of the Town were directed by his [Hildersham's] Judgement, and so continued, and yet do continue Presbyterianly affected'.*[40] A desire for the established church to follow a more Protestant line persisted within the town after the Restoration. In 1661 13 leading inhabitants petitioned the Countess of Huntingdon to appoint a Mr. Buxston as vicar, who *'was ordained by the Classis'.*[41]

In 1672 the houses of William Hood and of Thomas and Samuel Doughty were licensed as meeting houses.[42] These men had been active before this license was granted. A letter dated August 1671, mentioned *'Mr Doughty the nonconformist that lives in Mr Bell's house'.*[43] In October 1672 the churchwardens of Ashby were fined for failing to present at the church court one *Brinsley in the house of one William Hood or of some other p[er]son of Ashby...keeping a conventicle meeting assemblie or congregation unlawfull & there preaching without a licence'.*[44] William Hood, or his son, in 1689 became a school feoffee, and thus seems to have continued the tradition of nonconformist feoffees.[45]

In 1690 Ithiel Smart reported to the Earl of Huntingdon that some parishioners *'rudely to our great disturbance have left the church before all was don: several that staid before, since this grant of Liberty, would hasten out so soon as sermon was ended; I demanded the reason of this change in them, they told me that they formerly were afraid of being prosecuted if they had done so'.*[46] With the Act of Toleration those who disagreed with the prevailing orthodoxy of the Established Church had less reason to remain communicants and were able to follow their own beliefs separately.

What was the social composition of those who supported Puritanism? Among the 100 or so who refused communion in 1615 seventeen prefaced their names with 'Mr.' or 'Mrs.', but none of those excommunicated for persistent refusal was wealthy. Three couples, two men and a widow were excommunicated in 1620. Two of the men left inventories, totalling in one case £32, and in the other £7. One couple were regular recipients of money from the Overseers of the poor, and the widow and another couple occasionally received money from the same source. On the other hand it is clear from the Archdeaconry Court that Mrs. John Burrowes was a regular absentee from the church yet she was never excommunicated.

Similarly in the 1670s, one couple and two women were excommunicated for persistent absence from church. One woman was the wife of a man who was in 1670 assessed as owning one hearth,[47] and in 1671 was described as being £6-10-0 in arrears with his rent.[48] The occupation of the man who was excommunicated was variously described as 'thatcher' or 'labourer'. But William Hood, assessed in 1670 at two hearths, and Samuel Doughty, who could afford to send three sons to University, were not excommunicated.

Whether or not this implies that the courts, or the churchwardens, were biased against the poorer members of the community, it is apparent that the register of presentments for nonconformists does not indicate the social composition of Puritans or Dissenters.

Despite the *'unmatched spectacle'* of a hundred parishioners protesting in support of Mr. Hildersham in 1615, this still leaves perhaps five hundred adults in the town that did not. What effects did the succession of Puritan ministers have on these men?

Hildersham drew attention to the contrast within the town which was *'famous among the Churches of Christ for the religious observance of the Sabbath day. And to this day...I dare say it is little or nothing behind any other Church in the countrey...yet shall you hardly finde in any place more Atheist recusants, more that doe seldome or never come to Church, that do so ordinarily and consistently serve the Devill in the Ale house, when we are serving God here in his house, than are to be found in this Towne'.*[49]

The town regulations, inspired by Ashby's Puritan leadership, were strict in prohibiting both trade and idleness on the Sabbath. No *'butchers, shoomakers, mercers nor any...* [other traders?] *...whatsoever'* were to sell anything except under a case of *'extra-ordinarie necessitie'*. No-one was to load his horse or mare with corn, grain, or anything else on the Sabbath, and no pipers or minstrels were allowed in the town then. Householders were ordered to stop anyone from playing cards, dice or *'tables'* on the Sabbath, and no-one was permitted to play *'Bowles, foot ball, hand ball, or any other games'* then.[50]

Of course Sabbath bylaws are not necessarily indicative of a persistent Puritan bias within the parish. But it is significant that these bylaws were enforced. In 1583 two men were prosecuted for *'keping theire shopp wyndows open to sell meate on a Sunday'*. In 1612 John Draper and his son were presented for gathering apples upon the Sabbath, and ten years later Hugh Nikolson *'wrought on the Sabbath'*.[51]

Visitors to the town were not exempt. In 1612 a fletcher was prosecuted for travelling on the Sabbath to sell his wares,[52] and in 1628 the constable recorded that he had received 2/10 in fines *for a pedler a cotler and a parmonger for traviling of the Sabath day'*. Three years later ten shillings was extracted from *'2 men with carriages that brought wine to the town on ye Sabbath'*, and in the following year 1/10 was extracted from *'a poore man yt travelath to sell pares upon ye Sabaith'*.[53]

But it was the alehouse that seems to have caused most concern to the Puritan minded members of the community. Alehouses were, first, the sources of much gossip and sometimes of cases for defamation. In 1634 Richard Smith visited William Pight's house *'to drinke a Jugg of beare...and told this depo[*nent*] that he could tell him a pretty Jest...that Nicholas Sikes kisses Robert Hassard's wife as often as her husband.'* [54]

Alehouses were also the scenes of drunkenness and disorder. In 1614 Thomas Taylor was prosecuted for keeping disorderly company in his house, and Thomas Heywood for frequenting disorderly company on the Sabbath. The latter complained that he had merely gone *'to paie a poor man his wags for worke done to buy him vittualls'*.[55] In 1630 four Ashby men were brought before the Archdeaconry Court on account of an obscene practical joke that they had played upon a young man who was *'beastly drunk'* in the house of William Rogers.[56]

In particular the alehouse often proved more attractive than the Church. In 1630 John Heape was presented for drinking in an alehouse during morning prayers on the Sabbath.[57] In the same year Laurence Child was prosecuted for keeping company drinking in his house during evening prayers *'the which company could not be knowne because...ye said churchwardens comeing to ye said house to see what disorders were then & there, the said company ran away.'* [58]

As Chalmers concluded, Puritanism led to a *'more aggressive application of Sabbatarian and moralising regulations within the parishes, reflected in the churchwardens' presentments.* [59]

It is interesting that in 1625 when the Blackfordby chapelwardens presented Isabell, the wife of William, Joyce for being a recusant papist, they concluded the presentment by stating that she *'was p[re]sented before by us and we were p[ro]mised to have an excomm[unicat]ion against her but we have none and therefore yt is to no purpose to p[re]sent her in this court'.*[60] The chapelwardens themselves were in this case more extreme than the church court.

It is probably significant that the number of men prosecuted for drunkenness and profaning the Sabbath declined as the vicars became less Puritanical. Some prosecutions continued. In 1671 Thomas Ashpinshaw senior was prosecuted at the church court for drunkenness and John Draper for drunkenness and blaspheming. In the following year two of the leading inhabitants of the town, David King and Simon Perrin, were prosecuted for brawling in the vestry during a parish meeting.[61]

For several years in the 1690s and in the early years of the eighteenth century, the churchwardens reported simply that *'omnia bene'*. This was, of course, a reflection of the declining influence of the Archdeaconry Courts. But fines continued to be imposed upon absentees from church until 1686; on failure to pay church levies for another twenty years after that; and prosecutions for adultery and illegitimate children continued throughout the period.

These last two offences pose the question as to whether the Puritan ministers made the town more moral, or did they drive immorality underground, but were zealous in exposing it?

Over the period 1570-1720 only 65 baptisms were specifically recorded in the parish registers as being of illegitimate children, and there were a further eight burials of bastards, whose dates of baptism are unknown. This formed 1% of the total baptisms in the town. Thirteen of these baptisms took place in the six decades when Puritanism in Ashby was at its height. Thirty seven occurred in the six decades after the Restoration of the monarchy.

There were of course many ways of removing an illegitimate child from the parish. In 1637 Ralph Narborough of Ashby was prosecuted for assisting Isabell Goodrich of Coleorton to avoid the legal consequences of her adultery with Humphrey Wood. Narborough's crime was that he had allowed his victualling house to be used as a meeting place between the mother and one John Lyon, who, for £5 - of which he later complained that he had only received two - took away the child. Before the case reached the Archdeaconry Court the child was dead.[62]

The numbers of prosecutions for immoral offences at the church courts are noteworthy. Between 1570 and 1630 26 couples were presented for fornication before marriage, 17 for a *common fame* of fornication, and six women or couples for producing illegitimate children. The corresponding figures for the years 1660 to 1720 are 11, 4 and 15.

Thus the numbers prosecuted for producing illegitimate children increased in the second period, but fewer were prosecuted for adultery before marriage. The latter may have been the result of a closer scrutiny, in the earlier period, of the number of weeks between marriage and childbirth. In 1609 two couples were prosecuted who had had children within 34 and 32 weeks of their marriages. In 1620 Thomas Pestell wrote to the Court in favour of the victim of one zealous churchwarden: *'Sir, this poor fellow was somthing rigorously dealt w[i]thall in that the churchwarden being a witherd bachelour & not knowing w[ha]t belongs to the maine point of matrimonie woud needs p[re]sent him for that his wife went not full forty weeks, whereof those that kept strict account say she wanted not 3 and 2 I have heard say the law allows a mayd.*[63]

But the principal conclusion is clear. The attitude towards immorality appears to have been much stricter before 1630 than afterwards. The Puritans did not make the town more moral, but they did expose immorality more zealously than did their successors. Chalmers compared the presentments for all the parishes of Leicestershire in the period up to 1633 and concluded that *'It is significant that far from being reticent upon all matters the presentments of Ashby parish were, on matters of immorality, violation of the sabbath and incontinence fuller than the presentments from other parishes of less puritan outlook'.*[64]

Perhaps the best example of the social pressures of Puritanism upon the life of the parish is revealed in a petition to the Bishop of Lincoln from Richard Spencer, an Ashby chandler. When Brinsley, as curate of Ashby, was asked *'to publish & demaund in the church certaine mony of his the said Spencers w[hi]ch was taken owte of his house...when his howse was on fire and after burned downe to the grownd w[i]th all his goods to the valew of xl*[li] *the said Mr Brinsley answered nay, nay, the crosse hath lighte on the & a wors Judgment hangeth ov[er] thy head, thow wilte have thy children baptised w[i]th ye crosse & the said Spencer answered that yf he had anie more children he would have them baptised w[i]th the signe of the crosse according to his ma[jes]ties laws,...afterwards Mr Hildersham in his sermon said that there was three dwelling houses burned & two of them were Christians & the third meaning the s[ai]d Spencer, he could not tell what to make of him...Also Mr Hildersham's wife came to a widowe woman where the fire began & told her Jone be of good comforte iiii*[li] *will build upp thy howse againe, & as for Spencer the crosse hath lighte on him, let him beware the surplesse.*[65]

We do not know of Hildersham or Brinsley's response to this petition, but it does appear that the public condemnation of those who were deemed irreligious, such as Spencer, made life uncomfortable for all who would not conform to the piety demanded from the pulpit.

III. THE MINISTERS OF ASHBY 1632-1720

The vicars who succeeded Hildersham were not all unsympathetic to Puritanism. As we have seen, one of the ministers brought into the living during Hildersham's third suspension, Thomas Pestell, was a moderate with Puritan tendencies. Similarly Pestell's successor, Anthony Watson, who was vicar from 1622, was a moderate who was in 1635 prosecuted for various Puritan sympathies. He excused himself for not wearing a surplice by saying that he did not wear it occasionally *'when he could not come att the surples & when the same hath binn washing'*. He had given communion to standing parishioners only in the case of two old and impotent people who had been unable to kneel, except that sometimes *'in a multitude he might occasionally (but did never willingly) admi[ni]ster the same to others sitting'*.[66]

Watson did not gain the respect of all his parishioners. In 1637 Joseph Hatterley was prosecuted *'for raileing upon Mr Watson...in the open streets there w[i]th irreverent words...in contempt of his place & p[er]son.'*[67] In 1635 Clement Wakelyn, aged only 14, was alleged to have said *'give me a pot of ale Ile give thee a tost etc'* during one service.[68] One year later William Wakelyn kept his hat on his head during the sermon, saying he *'cared neither for God nor the devill'*.[69] John Draper, senior, was also presented for misbehaving in church *'by reson of taking too much drinke before'*.[70]

Little is known about the religious life of Ashby during the Civil War although it may be noticed that, like the schoolhouse, which probably stood nearby, *'the viccaridg hous...was in the Late warrs pulled downe'*.[71]

The death of Ithiel Smart in 1661 occasioned the petition which has already been mentioned, in favour of Mr. Buxston, lately of Staffordshire, an able and fit man of forty, *'ordained by the Classis'*. Of the 13 signatories to this petition only 2 or 3 are known to have had any links with nonconformity but all were leading inhabitants of the town, and most, if not all, served as town officers.

But the choice of Ashby's vicar belonged to the Hastings family, and no vicar was to be presented who had not been regularly ordained. The Countess of Huntingdon, acting on behalf of her son the seventh Earl, appointed Alexander Jones and not Mr Buxston.

Alexander Jones' incumbency is significant because Jones seems to have been the first vicar to try to end amicably a dispute that had lasted for over ninety years. The claim of Blackfordby men that they were neither bound to worship at Ashby church, nor to pay levies for its repair, but that the vicar of Ashby was bound to take services in

Blackfordby chapel, dated from the end of the sixteenth century. The Blackfordby men, and several Ashby men, declared that there were only sufficient pews at St Helen's for Ashby people, and any Blackfordby men who came *'weare inforced to stand as other strangers did.'* Ashby, moreover, had a fund for repairing the church, and contributions from Blackfordby in the past had been entirely voluntary. The conversion of this fund to maintain a school in Ashby was further evidence that Blackfordby men were not parishioners of Ashby, for witnesses had never *'hard that it was to such use converted by the consents or agreement of the inhabitants of Blougherby'*.[72]

Throughout the first forty years of the seventeenth century the inhabitants of Blackfordby complained about the lack of services at Blackfordby – for example, in 1615 *'they have noe minister nor haue had any service for the space of halfe a yere last past'*, by reason of the neglect of the Ashby vicar.[73] The latter claimed that he was only bound to serve Blackfordby as *'the cure of a chapell of ease is by lawe to be served'*.[74] This quarrel continued in the 1630s, when the chapelwardens regularly presented the vicar for failing to serve the chapel adequately, while the latter periodically presented the chapelwardens for failing to join the perambulation of the parish.

In 1663 Alexander Jones and inhabitants of both Blackfordby and Ashby signed an agreement. It settled the specific dispute over how far Blackfordby people were liable to pay levies for Ashby church. In future the inhabitants of Blackfordby were liable to pay one-sixth of all the charges of maintaining the church and churchyard in Ashby, but not for the beautifying of the church, nor for the upkeep of the clock and chimes.

But within fourteen years the general problem of the chapelry's status arose again with a dispute concerning liability to pay poor rates, and a year later an additional dispute arose over whether burials were allowed in the chapel. A final solution was only reached two centuries later when Blackfordby was made into a separate parish.

Despite his failure to end the quarrel between Blackfordby and Ashby, Alexander Jones was a popular vicar. When, in 1671, the Countess of Huntingdon decided to transfer him to another parish, 97 parishioners petitioned the Earl to persuade the Countess to change her mind.[75] This petition was supported by virtually all the leading townspeople, and Mr. Jones was persuaded to *'resigne up Piddletowne'* and asked his patron for permission to stay in the parish: *'The parish of Ashby, as soone as the Gentleman Mr Knight sent to supply his roome, came… did then with so general a Concurrence and earnest importunity desire my stay that at length I did give them fair hopes.'*[76]

But the opinions of the vicar and parish were simply ignored and Mr Jones was replaced.

The power of the patron was absolute. In 1690 Ithiel Smart complained that *'my burthen is to heavy'*, but that he had not made any financial arrangements to ease his worries *'for I woud doe nothing w[ith]out Y[our] L[ordship]'s order'.*[77] In the same year Mr. Smart rushed to explain to the Earl that he had made a minor change *'not upon choice, or to humor any party, but to keep some that rudely, to o[u]r great disturbance have left the church before all was don'* and he added that *'they would not stay unless I concluded in the Desk I made trial and since not one has gon out til the whole service has ended.'* Nevertheless if the Earl disapproved Mr. Smart was quick to assure him that he would promptly return to his former practice.[78] The Earl apparently did disapprove, for sixteen days after his earlier letter Mr. Smart reported that he had conformed and *'some went out of the Church, but I matter not their cavils, nor doe their censures weigh with me: It is Y[our] L[ordship]'s favour that I covet.'*[79]

Three years later John Lord, the new vicar, wrote to give his consent to the conditions which the Earl had laid down. *'Your Lordship's propositions are soe fair and commendable that I cannot but approove them'.*[80] In brief, Mr. Lord promised to read the communion service before and after the sermon at the altar, to wear a surplice in the pulpit, to perform the churching of women at the communion table, and to ensure that bodies were brought into church during burial services.

As the third Earl was responsible for the Puritanism of the parish early in this period, so the seventh Earl was responsible for the presentation of conforming ministers such as John Lord and Ithiel Smart, the younger. The importance of this control must not be underestimated. Although the dogma of religion may have influenced only a few in the parish, the vicar in the pulpit and the town officers in the manorial court could force the majority to comply with that dogma, which might include every aspect of social behaviour. And both the church and the manorial court were controlled by the patron and lord of the manor, the Earl of Huntingdon.

# ELEVEN

## *The manorial lord & the town community*

IN the preceding chapters, there have been many references to the power of the lord of the manor. This may partly be because so much manorial material has survived in the Hastings' manuscripts. But in seventeenth century Ashby, as in many other small market towns, the Church and the Manor were the most powerful institutions. What was the extent of the powers of the lord of the manor and in what ways did seventeenth century Ashby operate as a community?

### I. THE LORD OF THE MANOR

The religious influence of the lord of the manor, as patron of the living, has already been described. The fact that Ashby had a series of Puritan ministers was the direct result of the influence of the third Earl. The Earl's successors showed little enthusiasm for Puritanism. In the short term, this had a more direct effect upon Arthur Hildersham, who, unprotected, was suspended several times, than upon the town as a whole.

Of course, the influence of the patron was directly effective only when there was a vacancy in the living. But at such times they could, and did, ignore the wishes of the parishioners; and the man whom they chose to appoint was secure in his living as long as he carried out the wishes of his patron. The popularity of Alexander Jones did not prevent him from being transferred to another parish. Ithiel Smart in his correspondence, and John Lord by his promises before taking up office, demonstrate the power that was enjoyed by the seventh Earl.

By selecting a vicar who conformed to their opinions the Earls could ensure that the religious life of the parish was under their influence.

Similarly the third Earl tried to ensure that the education that was provided in the parish conformed to his beliefs. In 1567 Ashby Grammar School was given a legal foundation, and responsibility for running it was handed over to trustees, who were selected to mirror the Earl's convictions. The similarity of the 1575 Ashby *Statutes and Orders* with those drawn up in 1574 for Leicester School suggests that both were written under the Earl's direct influence. The Hastings' influence over Ashby school during the seventeenth century was limited. Puritan, or non-conformist, schoolmasters were appointed by self-perpetuating feoffees, and not by successive Earls. Nevertheless, the school tenants' petition of 1682 was addressed to the Earl of Huntingdon asking that school rents should not be increased.[1] The feoffees were in favour of a modest increase in rents, but the tenants believed that the feoffees could be persuaded not to demand these increases if the Earl so wished.

Towards the end of the seventeenth century there was a concerted attempt by the 3rd Earl's successors to restrict the feoffees' powers. Mr. Jaques, in a letter to the 7th Earl in 1685, stated that '*Mr. Piddocke has drawn an Instrument for the feoffees of this schoole to signe, to resigne their trust of choosing the schoole Mr for the time to come to Y[our] H[onour] and Y[our] most noble family: Mr Smart offers to signe first and I doubte not but all or most of the feoffees will follow however I intend to goe with Mr Piddocke to all of them*'.[2] In the same year a petition, according to Nicholas Carlisle, was presented to Lord Chancellor Jeffries, attacking the feoffees for financial mismanagement.[3] One example of this was that George Swindell's house was rented from the feoffees at £2 a year, while Swindell was subletting those parts of the house which he was not occupying at £19 a year. As a result of this petition, Carlisle continued, Jeffries ordered the Earl of Huntingdon to have the future nomination of every schoolmaster. Although the feoffees seem to have selected Mr. Save and Mr. Lynes in 1695 in the same way as they selected their predecessors, they may well have been prompted by the Earl. Scott maintains that the Earls appointed all the Headmasters from 1685-1803, when the Court of Chancery resolved that this power should be returned to the feoffees.[4]

The Earls could easily exert pressure on the townspeople in general through the manorial court to which almost all of the inhabitants owed suit and which was the jurisdiction that was most active in governing the daily life of the people of the area. The court was summoned through the Earl's bailiff and presided over by his steward. The bailiff probably chose the jury, and the jury elected the town's officers. Just as the Earl might influence the selection of churchwardens by his control over the vicar; the lord of the manor, through his bailiff and steward, could exercise a considerable influence in the selection of the town officers.

The manorial court might be used more directly to further the lord's interests. Two specific rules were included in the set of bylaws to safeguard the lord's income. As noted above, it was ordered that corn should be brought into the open market and not sold in private, and that horses were not to be loaded and to go down the back streets in order to defraud the lord's officers of his toll.[5] The case of Job Smith, the tenant of the lord of Seal, against whom the Earl of Huntingdon was engaged in a law suit, suggests that the lord of Ashby manor was not above using the manorial court to satisfy his private feelings.[6]

The Earls of Huntingdon exercised social leadership within the town. The inclusion in the Hastings' family papers of some of the accounts drawn up by the Overseers of the Poor and the churchwardens suggests that these officers, who were not responsible to the manorial court, nevertheless exercised their powers under the scrutiny of the lord.

Members of the Hastings family gave regular amounts to help the poor of the parish. Tenants in distress looked to the Earl and his family for help. In 1663, the widow of Ithiel Smart (mother of the man who became vicar in1676) asked the Earl or his mother for help in silencing *'ye bespattering toung of y[ou]r servant Job Brookes'*.[7] It was also to the Earl that John Elton appealed when he had *'Suffered much abuse by three neighbours'*.[8] Finally, it was to the Earl of Huntingdon that an Ashby man in 1739 appealed for help in rectifying wrongs that had been done to him and his mother seventeen years previously.[9]

The lord of the manor's presence was of great economic importance to the traders of the town. Some examples of Ashby traders who were patronized by the Hastings family have already been given. To these examples may be added two more. John Bowler was an Ashby glazier who was frequently employed at the castle. In 1615 £7-10-8 was paid to him as the *'remender'* of his bill. In 1629 he acted as both glazier and plumber in lining the *'Cesterne'* with lead, mending the pipes *'that brought water to the house w[hi]ch were often stopt'* and glazing the gatehouse and the larder. For this he and his helpers were paid £15. The following year he cast the lead in *'the litle room w[i]thin the best chamber'* and put in new glass there and in the room below, for which he and his workpeople received almost £4. Later in the same year he received £2-8-8 for *'remoueinge and mendinge all the pipes that carry water from the ponds to the brewhouse lawndrie & dairy'*.[10]

Abraham Ashe profited from the fact that so many people lived in so small a town. Ashe was a shoemaker and in March 1615 was paid eleven shillings for boots and shoes that he had supplied to members of the Earl's household. In the following January he received 24/- for three pairs of boots that he had made for the Earl, and five months later received a further ten shillings for repairing the Earl's boots. In the same month he was also paid four shillings for two pairs of shoes for the Earl's footmen and during 1616 two bills totalling almost £3 were paid, for shoes and *'underlaying'* the Earl's boots. Twenty years later Ashe was still employed in making shoes and boots for the Earl and his household. His bill in 1638 included slippers and a pair of *'spanish lether'* shoes for the Earl, *'stronge winter bootes'* for *'henery the coacheman'*, a pair of *'pumps for the postestilliane boy'* and some *'french hele'* shoes for Thomas Cundie.[11]

In this respect, the presence of the Earl's household was at least as important to Ashby traders as that of the Earl himself. In 1609 68 servants were entitled to sup at the lord's table daily, and Claire Cross observed that most of the servants of the 3rd Earl's household were local.[12]

The Earl's economic influence upon the town could also be exercised in a less direct manner. The grant of markets in 1613 may have been partly because Ashby was under the Earl's particular care and protection. The men of Leicester realized that, to gain the Earl's favour, they had only to offer concessions *'for Ashbye gloovars'*. The Justices of the Peace also realized the particular authority of the Earl in Ashby when they were asked to suppress some Ashby alehouses in 1627 and, as noted above, resolved not to use their own authority, but to request the help of the Earl *'in respecte of his beinge Lord of the said Towne, And of his muche residence there.'*

The Earl as Lord Lieutenant of Leicestershire may have been able to use his influence in favour of Ashby men more directly. John Holland of Ashby was in 1616 given the task of clothing the men that were sent to Ireland, for which he received almost £50. Holland also shared a contract worth £123 for clothing the 150 men who were sent to Bohemia in 1625. In 1627 Holland was again commissioned to clothe 150 men despatched on an expedition against Calais.[13]

Ashby was a frequent meeting place for the local militia, and in 1624 it was the rendezvous for the force sent to Bohemia from Leicestershire. The Earl may have been able to favour Ashby men when Leicestershire had to send troops abroad. Although Ashby and Loughborough contributed almost equal numbers of men to the county militia which stayed at home, Loughborough had, in 1624, to send eleven men to Bohemia while Ashby sent only two.[14] No Ashby man was conscripted for the levies in 1625.

The influence of the Earls of Huntingdon in Leicestershire depended upon the obedience of their tenants. In Parliamentary elections the Ashby voters did not cause any trouble. In 1688 Mr. Jaques assured the Earl that the Ashby freeholders would not vote until they had waited upon the Earl, to ask his advice.[15] Two years later Mr. Piddocke informed the Earl that he could get those Ashby freemen who had served their apprenticeship in Leicester to use their votes satisfactorily.[16] In an election in 1719, eighteen years after the death of the Jacobite seventh Earl, 43 out of the 47 Ashby voters voted for the Jacobite candidate.[17]

The Earls of Huntingdon largely controlled the agrarian economy of Ashby. Although one-quarter of the town area was common land over which the Earl had no direct control, much of the rest was demesne. The release of most, if not all, of this demesne land in the second half of the seventeenth century aggravated the decline in Ashby rents, and the manner in which this land was let affected the social structure of the town by allowing the growth of large farms.

In addition, the Hastings family owned all the mills in the town, and the inhabitants of Ashby were prohibited from taking corn to be ground elsewhere. In 1640 William Beadley, a miller from outside the town was prosecuted for conspiring to grind Ashby corn. The defendants' plea that the Ashby mills were insufficient to grind all of the town's corn was discounted and the Earl's monopoly confirmed.[18] In 1654 William Hazard of Ashby formally promised to suppress his querns, or hand-mills.[19] In 1737 this monopoly was still in force, for in that year twenty-two inhabitants, perhaps the owners of alehouses, signed an undertaking that they would grind *all the malt brued* in their houses at the Earl's malt mill. Only two people were listed as refusing to sign this undertaking.[20] From about 1660, the mills ceased to be directly controlled by the Earl, but were leased out to other men who worked the monopoly for their own benefit.

The effects of the absence of the Earls of Huntingdon after 1660 illustrate the extent of Ashby's dependence upon the Earl's patronage. The absence of the lord was not the only cause of the economic depression in the town at this time. But the destruction of the castle meant that Ashby men such as John Bowler were no longer required to repair its fabric, while the removal of the family to Castle Donington probably meant that Ashby craftsmen, such as Abraham Ashe, were not used to the same extent. The enclosure and leasing out of the demesne land was probably the result both of the Hastings' financial difficulties and their departure from the town.

There are other indications that the period after 1645 marks the start of a decline in the power that the Earls exercised in Ashby. It seems clear that George Smith was able to embezzle money from the Oakthorpe mines during the 1660s because the coal accounts were not regularly scrutinized, and Smith knew this. His dishonesty only came to the attention of the Hastings family after allegations from Turner, who was probably the manager of another of the Earl's mines.[21]

There are also indications that the Earl's social influence in the town was declining. Samuel Shaw persuaded three local gentlemen to give him money to rebuild Ashby School, but none of these was a Hastings. It is difficult to conceive in the first half of the century of a major charitable scheme in the town not receiving some attention, and, probably, a contribution, from the Earl or his family.

All the schools that were founded in the town after 1660 were founded by private individuals - by William Langley; by a consortium of townspeople which included Isaac Dawson; and, later in the eighteenth century, by Alderman Newton of Leicester.[22]

The Hastings family in the eighteenth century seem to have had less religious influence. Selina, Countess of Huntingdon, one of the leading patrons of the Methodist Movement, lived at a house erected close to the ruins of Ashby castle. But when George Whitefield, one of her protégés, visited the town a riot occurred in front of her house. Whitefield subsequently wrote: *'Ungrateful Ashby! O that thou knewest the day of thy visitation. ...What avails throwing pearls before swine who only turn again and rend you?'* [23]

The only member of the Hastings family who subsequently showed any great interest in the town was Lord Moira who early in the nineteenth century developed the Ashby-de-la-Zouch canal, and tried to turn Ashby into a spa. His death, in 1826, together with the sale of most of the Hastings' property in Ashby, marks the end of the close connection between the town and the Hastings family.

So, in at least three ways, the power of the Hastings family was declining from the end of the Civil War. Religious toleration made the right of patronage less important. The economic dominance of the Hastings declined considerably with the departure of the family, and with the increase, during the eighteenth century, of larger farmers. Finally, the power of the manorial lord decayed as the manorial institutions decayed. The lord's control over the election to manorial offices ceased to be important when the offices themselves became unimportant. By the end of the eighteenth century a smaller proportion of the town owed suit to the manorial court, and it seems clear that the number of officers who treated their manorial obligations seriously had also declined.

## II. THE COMMUNITY OF ASHBY.

At the start of the seventeenth century the church, the market, and the manorial court served as the focal points for the community of the town.

A sense of community involves not only ideas of mutual aid, but also of public knowledge, and, if necessary, public condemnation; for mutual help implies mutual awareness of each other's needs. The manorial court served as one institution in which communal disapproval expressed itself in public punishment. But perhaps a better example, in so far as the punishments imposed by the manorial court were usually restricted to fines, is that provided by the church. Puritanism may have helped to foster the 'Protestant work ethic', but it also reflected an authoritarian sense of discipline where any immorality had to be publicly acknowledged. Adulterers had to stand in a hair cloth outside the church before the service, and in the middle of the aisle when the service had begun. They had to face the congregation until the homily concerning adultery had been read, at which they had to abase themselves on the ground, declare their guilt and ask publicly for forgiveness. Rose Jackson of Ashby, who was in 1619 found guilty of defaming the wife of John Bowler, was forced to confess her faults before the whole town and ask forgiveness.[24]

Within the community a hierarchy upheld public virtue. As the manorial officers enforced the bylaws, the churchwardens and vicar supervised the religious and moral life of the parish. Their authority was not to be questioned and bylaws were enacted against men who obstructed or threatened the town officers. Hildersham declared that *'Hearers ought not to dispute against any truth revealed of God, by their Minister, though it bee contrary to their reason and humour'.*[25] Joseph Hatterley was brought before the Archdeaconry Court because he had addressed the vicar *'in contempt of his place & p[er]son, Watson Watson diu[er]s times without adding anie title of respecte belonginge to his degree in schooles or to his office in the Church'.*[26]

The sense of community was displayed by the acceptance of responsibility on behalf of the town to help its poorer members. An element of selfishness may explain the free distribution of *'pooder'* to the poor at a time of plague as an attempt to prevent disease from entering the town.[27] But such explanations do not explain the generosity in other cases. In less than four years Ann Sansom, a cripple, received from the Overseers of the Poor almost £3-10-0 in five single sums. There was no direct need to help with the schooling of Simon, the son of Mr. Thomas Perrins, but money was laid out every year for five years for this purpose.[28] There was no need for men and women to stipulate in their wills that part of their money should be used to help the poor, but many people did so. At least eight substantial charities to educate or feed or apprentice the poor were set up between 1660 and 1725. Such charities were founded because of the general belief that the richer members of the community had an obligation to help the poorer.

This same principle is reflected in many of the manorial rules, for example, the rights of cottagers being upheld by a separate cottiers' pasture. But the poor were not simply set apart from the rich. Fern and bracken were important commodities that grew upon the waste land - mainly, at this time, on the Woulds. This commodity was not let out for the profit of a single individual nor was there a 'free-for-all' in which the poorer would go short. Instead it was ordered that no-one was to mow any of the fern or bracken until July 26th; no-one was to start mowing until sunrise upon that day, and, finally, that no-one was to employ more than two mowers in one day.

As Joan Thirsk put it, '*Common fields and pastures kept alive a vigorous co-operative spirit in the community*'.[29] The town fields required communal rules to prevent the damage of one person's property by the carelessness of another. The formulation and enforcement of these rules was in the hands of a manorial court that was, essentially, oligarchical and, on occasion, the manorial court had to be prompted through an extraordinary town meeting or petition. But the townsmen had sufficient confidence to address their opinions to the manorial court in order to change their rules, rather than to attempt unilateral action without the court's consent. The court agreed to petitions both to reduce the stints for the fallow field, and to lay the commons together.

Four specific examples may illustrate the sense of community in Ashby during this century. First, it has been noted that there were several petitions to the lord of the manor which carried the agreement of a large proportion of the town's population. In particular, the petition in favour of Mr. Jones staying as vicar of Ashby was supported by 97 names. Fourteen of these were of women, and this suggests that the petitioners may have been householders. If this is the case, the petition secured the express approval of one-third of the town.[30]

Secondly, in a single five-year period, at least 71 people played some part in administering the town, either as manorial officers or as jurymen. This figure does not include those who acted as church officers, Overseers of the Poor or of the Highways, or as school feoffees or trustees of any of the town charities. Thus almost one-third of the families in the town had members who were actively involved in its administration – a degree of popular participation and of communal obligation which has rarely if ever existed since.

Thirdly, the community in Ashby clubbed together against a common threat. In 1615 a hundred parishioners followed Hildersham in defying the church authorities. In 1685 Mr. Jaques reported that *'many tennants threaten to leave their grounds at next Lady Day except they have abatements'.*[31] Four years later Mr. Piddocke stated that *'there was a conspiracy amongst divers of ye ten[a]nts about flinging up grounds and getting Abattments'.*[32]

The final example of the sense of community in Ashby occurred sixty years before the rent conspiracies. Richard Spencer's petition to the Bishop of Lincoln concerning his treatment by Hildersham and Brinsley when his house was burned down has already been quoted at length. This incident is illuminating for several reasons. The light it sheds on how the Puritan leaders of the town ostracised those who did not follow their teachings has already been mentioned.

It also reminds us of the dangers of fire when most houses were half-timbered and many were probably thatched. But the fact that Spencer had asked Brinsley to *'publish & demaund in the church certaine mony'* that was stolen from his house at the time of a fire is a good example of the way in which the pulpit was used for matters of general, but not specifically ecclesiastical, interest. It also illustrates Spencer's attitude towards the town community to whom he appealed for help. It is worth emphasising that the petition itself was not concerned with the return of stolen money, or of repairing his house, but with the treatment that Spencer had received from Hildersham, Hildersham's wife and from Brinsley. Spencer felt that his position in the community was threatened by the way in which Ashby's religious leaders had treated him.

Of course these four examples do not show that every inhabitant felt himself a part of the community. The petition about Mr Jones was not signed by more than half the townsfolk. Two-thirds of the families did not take an active part in the town's affairs, even though those who did claimed to act in the name of the whole community. Anthony Watson took it upon himself in 1632 to speak *'in the name of the whole town'* when he enquired at the Archdeaconry Court about the wages of the parish clerk.[33]

The three town institutions - the church, the manorial court and the market – all flourished through much of the seventeenth century.

At the end of the sixteenth century Blackfordby men testified that Ashby church was full to overflowing with the inhabitants of Ashby alone, and that the Blackfordby men *'weare inforced to stand as other strangers did'.*[34] An inspection of St Helen's church in 1637 demonstrated the pressures on space when it complained that seats had been built in the middle aisle *'w[hi]ch straighten the passage, make it but three q[uarte]r of a yard wide in some p[ar]ts w[hi]ch formerly was (as still the belower p[ar]t is) about three yards wide.'*[35] To seat his scholars at church towards the end of the century Samuel Shaw had to build a gallery.[36]

In 1691, 54 freeholders and 239 other tenants owed suit to the manorial court and in May of that year only 53 failed to appear. Probably every family was represented at this court, and over 80% of those who owed suit attended.[37]

Attendance at the market was not compulsory, nor was it a formal occasion. But it was in the market place that most of the inns and alehouses were situated, and at market time these were the busiest social centres. Moreover it was through the market place on market days that criminals, such as James Moseley who was found guilty in 1693 of petty larceny, were whipped.[38]

All these focal points of the town community were to some extent controlled by the lord of the manor, and the presence of all these elements was typical of small market towns. Agricultural villages lacked a market, while the larger market towns were controlled by a Corporation rather than a manorial court.

By the end of the eighteenth century the three elements that had formed the focal points of the Ashby community in earlier times were in decay. In 1775 only 39 freeholders and 141 tenants were listed in the suit rolls of the manorial court – barely 35% of the total population.[39] The social power of the church had been broken by the growth of toleration, and there was an increasing social rift between church and chapel. Small market centres had been made less important through the improvement in communications, and a shift from trading in the open market to private transactions. Although the weekly markets continued, permanent shops became more important.

The destruction of the castle and the departure of the Hastings family in the previous century were major triggers in bringing about these changes. The enclosure and leasing out of the lord's lands enabled larger, more powerful farmers to emerge. The decline of the manorial court reflected the declining importance of the market and the enclosure of the old town fields, but it was also partly a result of the lord of the manor's absence. The Earl's social leadership in Ashby was, to some extent, taken over by men such as John Elton and Timothy Clarson. Elton's position in the town was unequalled in any earlier period outside the Earl's household. Hardly any Ashby man previously had possessed a personal fortune comparable with that of Timothy Clarson, a tanner, who died in 1718 leaving £1,000.[40] In time the rise of families such as the Piddockes, the Abnys and the Kirklands, created a social class that was largely distinct from the rest of the community.

But in 1700 this still lay in the future. The manorial court still functioned with regularity. Most people were members of the Church of England. Ashby market continued to be the trading capital for the immediate locality. The power of the manorial lord continued, and Ashby's inhabitants continued to live and work together in an ordered, hierarchical community.

Butter Cross
At the top end of Market Street, dismantled in 1827
*Courtesy of Ashby Museum*

# *Notes*

*B.M. = British Museum*
*H.L. = Huntington Library, California*
*L.M. = Leicester Museum Archives*
*L.R.O. = Leicestershire Records Office*
*P.R.O. = Public Records Office*
*T.L.A.H.S. = Transactions of Leicestershire Archaeological & Historical Society*
*V.C.H. = Victoria County History of Leicestershire*

FRONT COVER
L.R.O. DG 30/MA/249/3. This section forms less than 10% of the full map. It should be noted that the blank spaces in, for example, Market Street on this map do not indicate that there were no buildings there in 1735, but just that this land was held freehold and did not form part of the Earl of Huntingdon's property.

INTRODUCTION
1. *Agrarian History of England & Wales 1540-1640*, p.467. Peter Clark and Paul Slack suggest a similar number of market towns. Of these they define a little over 100 as being large market towns (with populations in 1500 of more than 1,500) and the remaining 600 or so as small market towns, like Ashby. *English Towns in Transition 1500-1700*, p. 9.
2. H.P.R. Finberg, *Approaches to History* (1962), p. 119.

CHAPTER 1: GEOGRAPHY & TOPOGRAPHY OF ASHBY
1. J. Mackay, *Journey through England* (2nd edition 1724), Vol II p. 166.
2. Ibid, p. 169.
3. W. Pitt, *General View of the Agriculture of the County of Leicestershire* (1813), p. 176.
4. H. L., HA Correspondence, 7744.
5. J.M.W.Laithwaite, in Papers given to the Vernacular Architecture Group, December 1969.

CHAPTER 2: MEDIAEVAL ASHBY
1. H.L., [Leicestershire Manorial Box 1]
2. Nichols, *History of Leicestershire* (1804), Vol. III p.561.
3. W. G. Hoskins, *The Midland Peasant* (1957), p.60.
4. W. G. Hoskins, *The Origin and Rise of Market Harborough* T.L.A.H.S. Vol. 25 p. 67.
5. Nichols, *History of Leicestershire* (1804), Vol. III pp.561-2.
6. G. Farnham, *Leicestershire Mediaeval Village Notes* (1933), Vol. VI pp.32-33.
7. G.H. Green & M.H. Green, *Loughborough Markets and Fairs* (1962), p. 15.

154

8. G. Farnham, op.cit., p. 36.

9. Ibid., p. 34

10. A. Hamilton Thompson, *The Building Accounts Of Kirby Muxloe, 1480-1484*, T.L.A.H.S., Vol. XI, p. 255.

11. Ibid., pp. 229 and 313.

12. John Ogilby, *Britannia* (1675), p. 169.

13. Claire Cross, *The Puritan Earl* (1966), p. 86.

14. H.L. [Leicestershire Manorial Box 3].


CHAPTER 3: DEMOGRAPHY

1. W.G.Hoskins, *Local History in England* (1959), p. 143.

2. Ibid., p.143. Anne Whiteman in *The Compton Census of 1676 – a Critical Edition* (1986) suggests a multiplier of 1.5 to translate the census return into total population, but the difference with Professor Hoskins' method is not significant.

3. V.C.H., Vol. III, p 145.

4. H.L., HAM Box 2, 5. A copy of this document is now at Ashby Museum. The Huntington Library has read the name as "Riche" rather than "Kirke". Humphrey Kirke was listed as an alehouse-keeper in 1627 and as a carpenter in a deposition in 1638. He signed his name with a mark and so was probably illiterate.

5. Jonathan Barry (editor), *The Tudor and Stuart Town, 1530-1688* (1990), p.12.

6. H.L., Hastings Miscellaneous Box 12, Overseers of the Poor Accounts 1628 – 1634. A copy of this document is now at Ashby Museum.

7. Vivian Salmon, *John Brinsley and His Friends*, T.L.A.H.S. Vol 51, p.8.

8. W. Scott, *The Story of Ashby-de-la-Zouch* (1907), p.91

9. L.R.O., BR II/18/15, f. 586, Leicester Borough Minute Book 1623-1625.

10. H.L., Hastings Miscellaneous Box 12, Churchwardens Accounts 1626 – 1636. A copy of this document is now at Ashby Museum.

11. *Calendar of State Papers Domestic, 1631-2*, p.161.

12. Martyn Bennett, *Henry Hastings and the Flying Army of Ashby de la Zouch*, T.L.A.H.S., Vol. 56 p. 68. W. Scott, *The Story of Ashby-de-la-Zouch* (1907), p.209.

13. Levi Fox, *A Country Grammar School –A History of Ashby-de-la-Zouch Grammar School* (1967), p.51.W. Scott, *The Story of Ashby-de-la-Zouch* (1907), p.382.

14. W. & J. Hextall, *Ashby-de-la-Zouch* (1852), p.94.

15. Nigel Goose, *Household size and structure in early-Stuart Cambridge* in Jonathan Barry (editor), *The Tudor and Stuart Town, 1530-1688* (1990), p.84.


CHAPTER 4: TRADE

1. L.R.O., DE 432/37

2. Staffordshire Records Office, Quarter Sessions, Roll 26, 9 James I.

3. P.R.O., E 134/ 13 Car.I, Mich. 43.

4. L.R.O., ES AB/9/1, f.10v.

5. H.L., 1615 Rental Roll [L1 K8, Box 61].

6. H.L., 1718 Rental Roll [non HMC Deeds, W Box 37]

7. W.G. Hoskins, *Provincial England* (1963), p.80.

8. Mary Bateson (ed.), *Leicester Borough Records 1509-1603* (1905), Vol. III p.411.

9. Helen Stocks (ed.), *Leicester Borough Records 1603-1688* (1923), p. 135.

10. Ibid., p.173.

11. Quoted by John Nichols, *History and Antiquities of the County of Leicester* (1795-1815), Vol. III, p.597.

12. H.L., [HA Accounts, Box 9, Accounts Book 1629-1631].

13. H.L., Hastings Miscellaneous Box 12, Household accounts 1638-1643. A copy of this document is now at Ashby Museum.

14. L.R.O., DE 432/37

15. Alan Everitt, "Marketing of Agricultural produce" in J. Thirsk (ed.) *Agrarian History of England 1540-1640* (1967), pp.559-561.

16. H.L., [LI K9, Box 62].

17. H.L., HAM Box 2.1 Book of Penal Laws. A copy of this document is now at Ashby Museum.

18. *The Diary of Richard Symonds*, (Camden Society 1859), p.178.

19. *Calendar of State Papers Domestic, 1644*, p.200.

20. Quoted by T. H. Fosbrooke, "Ashby-de-la-Zouch Castle", *Associated Arch. & Arch. Society Reports and Papers* (1911), Vol. 31.1, p.202.

21. H.L., [LI K8, Box 61].

22. *Calendar of Committee for Compounding*, I, p.270.

23. Quoted by Nichols, *Leicestershire*, III, p.611.

24. H.L., [LI K8 Box 61].

25. H.L., HA Correspondence, 5567.

26. *Calendar of State Papers Domestic, 1640*, p.450.

27. Ibid., 1644-5, p.544 and 1644, p.218.

28. *The Diary of Richard Symonds*, (Camden Society 1859), p.278.

29. *Calendar of Committee for Compounding*, II, p.1043.

30. L.M., ID 41/43/2-25.

31. Martyn Bennett *Leicestershire's Royalist Officers and the War Effort in the County 1642-1646*, T.L.A.H.S, Volume 59 p.45.

32. L.R.O., Quarter Sessions, QS 6/1/2, Court Order Book 1678-1700, pp. 55 & 55a.

33. L.R.O., Ashby parish papers, 4, Settlement certificates.

34. V.C.H., Vol. III, p.7.

35. Sir F.M. Eden, *The State of the Poor* (1797), Vol. II, p. 374.

36. G.H. & M.W. Green, *Loughborough Markets and Fairs* (1962), p.36.

37. P.R.O., WO 30/48

38. H.L., [LI K9 Box 64 and LI K8, Box 61].

39. H.L., HAM Box 3.29.

40. *Calendar of Committee for Compounding*, p.655.

41. H.L., Book of Penal Laws, HAM Box 2. A copy of this document is now at Ashby Museum.

42. H.L., HA Correspondence 7658.

43. H.L., HA Correspondence 7677.

44. H.L., HA Correspondence 7714.

45. H.L., HA Correspondence 7732.

46. H.L., HA Correspondence 7754.

47. H.L., HA Correspondence 7758.

48. H.L., HA Correspondence 10215.

49. H.L., HA Correspondence 10223.

50. H.L., HA Correspondence 10253.

51. H.L., HA Correspondence 7744.

52. H.L., HA Correspondence 2568.

53. H.L., HA Correspondence 7788.

54. H.L., HA Correspondence 10228.

55. H.L., Book of Penal Laws, HAM Box 2. A copy of this document is now at Ashby Museum.

56. H.L., HA Correspondence 7744.

57. H.L., HA Correspondence 7732.

58. H.L., HA Correspondence 7714.

59. H.L., HA Correspondence 7765.

60. H.L., HA Correspondence 10223.

61. H.L., HA Correspondence 10228.

62. H.L., HA Correspondence 10246.

63. Joan Thirsk, *"Tudor & Stuart Stamford"* in A. Rogers (ed.) *The Making of Stamford*, p. 72. Joan Thirsk also notes how public coaches appeared on London streets in Charles I's reign and by 1658 long distance coach services were available. By the end of the century the system of changing horses on the journey enabled passengers to travel fifty miles instead of 10-15 miles in a day.

64. H.L., [Coal Accounts, LIQ Box 1].

65. H.L., [Coal Accounts, LIQ Box 2].


CHAPTER 5: SOCIAL STRUCTURE & POOR RELIEF

1. W.G. Hoskins, *Provincial England* (1963), p.93. Peter Clark and Paul Slack use the subsidy assessments of the 1520s to reach a similar conclusion – that two-thirds of the urban population lived below, or very close to the poverty line. *English Towns in Transition 1500-1700* p. 112

2. For this and following paragraphs: H.L., Hastings Miscellaneous Box 12, 2. Overseers of the Poor Accounts 1628 – 1634. A copy of this document is now at Ashby Museum.

3. The following three paragraphs are based on H.L., Hastings Miscellaneous Box 12, 1. Churchwardens Accounts 1626-1636. A copy of this document is now at Ashby Museum.

4. H.L., [HA Accounts Box 8].

5. H.L., [Ibid., Box 15, Accounts Book 1640-1644].

6. H.L., [Ibid., Box 7].

7. Information in these two paragraphs is largely drawn from *Reports of the Commissioners for Inquiring concerning Charities*, (1838) 32, pt. V and Nichols, *Leicestershire*,Vol. III, pp 616-7.

8. In 1636/7 the Overseers of the Poor gave 5/- to Hugh Hall "*toward the makeinge of a monument for Ms. Right*".


CHAPTER 6: AGRICULTURE

1. J. Curtis, *Topographical History of Leicestershire*, p.4.

2. W.G. Hoskins, *Essays in Leicestershire History* (1959), p. 105.

3. H.L., [Leics. Manorial Box 1].

4. L.R.O. DG 30/MA/249/3.

5. In my thesis I failed to notice a reference in the Penal Laws to a fence between Drift Common and Ashby Woulds and incorrectly suggested that "Drift Common" might be an alternative name for "Near Common".

6. W.G.Hoskins, *The Midland Peasant* (1957), p.64.

7. H.L., [LI K8, Box 61]

8. Claire Cross, *The Puritan Earl* (1966), pp 79-80.

9. Claire Cross, *The Hastings Manuscripts*, T.L.A.H.S., Vol. XXXVIII, p.33.

10. H.L., [LI K8, Box 61] and H.L., [Manorial Folder, 67].

11. W. Pitt, *General View of the Agriculture of the County of Leicestershire* (1809), p.177.

12. Thomas Fuller, *The History of the Worthies of England* (1662), ii, p.126.

13. W. Lilly, *History of his Life and Times* (1715), p.8.

14. G. Farnham, *Leicestershire Mediaeval Village Notes* (1933), Vol. VI pp.32-33.

15. W.G.Hoskins, *The Midland Peasant* (1957), p.154.

16. L.R.O. and Lincoln Archives, Inventories used in following paragraphs.

17. W.G. Hoskins, *Essays in Leicestershire History* (1959), pp. 175-7.

18. H.L., *Book of Penal Laws*, HAM Box 2. A copy of this document is now at Ashby Museum.

19. H.L., HA Correspondence 2020.

20. H.L., HA Correspondence 7732.

21. H.L., HA Correspondence 7765.

22. H.L., HA Correspondence 7773.

23. H.L., HA Correspondence 10223.

24. H.L., HA Correspondence 10240.

25. H.L., HA Correspondence 10258.

26. H.L., HA Correspondence 7675.

27. H.L., HA Correspondence 7761.

28. H.L., HA Correspondence 7788.

29. H.L., HA Correspondence 7791.

30. H.L., HA Correspondence 10216.

31. H.L., HA Correspondence 10223.

32. H.L., [LI W2, Box 21].

33. H.L., [W Box 16].

34. *Calendar of State Papers Domestic 1640*, p.450.

35. H.L., [Leicestershire Manorial Box 29].


CHAPTER 7: HOUSING

1. Some of the information in this chapter is based on W.G. Hoskins: *The Midland Peasant* (1957) especially pages 283-299; and the *Historic Building Archaeological Survey* carried out in Ashby in 2004 by T.R. Projects on behalf of North West Leicestershire District Council

2. L.R.O., Inventories, 1585/62.

3. L.R.O., Inventories, 1584/99.

4. L.R.O., Inventories, 1586/126.

5. L.R.O., Inventories, 1590/177.

6. L.M., ID 41/13/11, f.91v.

7. L.R.O., Inventories, 1608/20.

8. L.R.O., Inventories, 1614/74.

9. L.R.O., Inventories, 1580/59 and 1581/59.

10. W.G. Hoskins, *The Midland Peasant* (1957), p.292.

11. Ibid., pp. 290-291.

12. L.R.O., Inventories, 1625/38.

13. L.R.O., Inventories, 1626/212.

14. H.L., HAM Box 2, 5. A copy of this document is now at Ashby Museum.

15. Lincoln Archives, Miscellaneous Correspondence, Cor/M/2, f.38.

16. H.L., Book of Penal Laws, HAM Box 2. A copy of this document is now at Ashby Museum.

17. W. Scott, *The Story of Ashby-de-la-Zouch* (1907), p.221. Scott may have simply copied this from W. & J. Hextall, *Ashby-de-la-Zouch* (1852), p.51.

18. H.L., Hastings Miscellaneous Box 7, item 4. A copy of this document is now at Ashby Museum.

19. W.G. Hoskins, *The Midland Peasant* (1957), p.301.


CHAPTER 8: LAW AND ORDER

1. L.R.O., DE 432/37

2. H.L., *Book of Penal Laws,* HAM Box 2. Much of the following pages relate to this document which covers 182 pages. A copy of this document is at Ashby Museum.

3. L.M., ID 41/13/50, f.147.

4. L.M. ID 41/13/80, f.117 and L.R.O., QS 7, Presentment Book 1

5. T.F.T. Plucknett, *A Concise History of the Common Law* (2nd edition 1936), p.95.

6. H.L., Overseers of the Poor Accounts 1628-1634, Hastings Miscellaneous Box 12. A copy of this document is now at Ashby Museum.

7. H.L., [LI K9 Box 64].

8. H.L., HA Correspondence, 7744 and 2568.

9. H.L., [LI K9 Box 64].

10. H.L. [Non-HMC Land Deeds, W Box 18].

11. W. Scott, *The Story of Ashby-de-la-Zouch* (1907), p. 272.

12. P.R.O., Depositions, E 134 Car I, Mich.43.

13. *Agrarian History of England & Wales 1540-1640* (1967), p.481.

14. L.R.O., QS 7/1.

15. L.R.O., ES/AB/9/1, f. 52.

16. H.L., [LI K9 Box 62].

17. H.L., [Leicestershire Local Affairs, Box 4].

18. H.L., [1718 Rental Roll, non HMC Deeds, W Box 37].

19. *Calendar of State Papers Domestic, 1631-2,* p.161.

20. Blackfordby Chapelwardens' accounts 1680-1780.

21. L.M., ID 41/14/4, f.39.

22. H.L., Overseers of the Poor Accounts 1628-1634, Hastings Miscellaneous Box 12. A copy of this document is now at Ashby Museum.

23. H.L., [Leicestershire Local Affairs Box 1].

24. L.R.O., QS 6/1/2, p. 190a and QS 5/1/1, p. 12a

25. H.L., 1661 Rental, [LI K9 Box 61].

26. L.R.O., DE 432/22

27. H.L., HA Correspondence, 3986.

28. L.R.O., QS 7/2, Michaelmas 6 William & Mary.

29. H.L., [Leicestershire Manorial Box 29].

30. L.M., ID 41/4/XLVII, f. 151.

31. L.M., ID 41/4/XXXIII, f. 107.

32. L.R.O., ES/AB/30, School enfeoffment.

33. H.L., [LI K9, Box 62].

34. P.R.O., E 179 240/279.

35. L.M., ID 41/4/XLVII, f.151.

36. H.L., [LI K9, Box 62].

37. H.L., [LI K9, Box 62].

38. H.L., [LI K9, Box 61].

39. Blackfordby Chapelwardens' accounts 1680-1780.

40. H.L., [LI K8, Box 61].

41. Both examples occur in H.L., [LI K9, Box 64].

42. H.L., [LI K9, Box 62] and W. Scott, *The Story of Ashby-de-la-Zouch* (1907), p.272.

43. W. & J. Hextall, *Ashby-de-la-Zouch* (1852), p.120.

CHAPTER 9: EDUCATION

1. L.R.O., ES/AB/29.

2. L.M., ID 41/4/273

3. A. White, *A History of Loughborough Endowed Schools* (1969).

4. L.R.O., Inventories for 1576.

5. Ibid. 1602/63.

6. Parish registers.

7. Ibid.

8. H.L., [W LI W2].

9. L.R.O., ES AB/9/2.

10. L.R.O., ES/AB/9/1.

11. L.R.O., Wills, 1695/77.

12. One of "The Lives of thirty-two English Divines" bound with S. Clarke, *Martyrology* (1660).

13. Most of the material re Hall and Chomeley is from John Jones, *Memoirs of Bishop Hall* (1826).

14. John Jones, *Memoirs of Bishop Hall* (1826), p.9.

15. *Report of the Charity Commissioners*, 32, part V, (Parliamentary Papers 1839, XV), pp. 346-7.

16. W. Lilly, *A History of His Life and Times* (1715), p.4.

17. J. Brinsley, *Ludus Literarius* (1612).

18. L.R.O., ES AB/9/2.

19. W. Lilly, *A History of His Life and Times* (1715), p.5.

20. Ibid., p.5.

21. Ibid., p.6.

22. Ibid., p.6.

23. Ibid., p.6.

24. L.M., ID 41/13/44.

25. W. Lilly, *A History of His Life and Times* (1715), p.3.

26. Ibid., p.6.

27. L.R.O., ES/AB/9/1, f.1.

28. Ibid., ff. 4 & 4v.

29. Ibid., f. 5v.

30. Levi Fox, *A Country Grammar School –A History of Ashby-de-la-Zouch Grammar School* (1967), p.6.

31. Claire Cross, *The Free Grammar School of Leicester* (1953), p.14.

32. A. White, *A History of Loughborough Endowed Schools* (1969), p.66.

33. L.R.O., ES AB/9/1, f. 4v.

34. P.R.O., C93 43/Inq/24/9.

35. *Report of the Charity Commissioners*, 32, part V, (Parliamentary Papers 1839, XV), p.336.

36. L.R.O., ES AB/9/1, f.48v.

37. Edmund Calamy, *An Account of the Ministers, Lecturers, Masters and Fellows of Colleges and Schoolmasters, who were ejected or silenced after the Restoration in 1660, by, or before, the Act of Uniformity* (2nd edition 1713) Vol II pp. 426-436.

38. Ibid., p. 429.

39. Ibid., p. 430.

40. Levi Fox seems to have followed Calamy in recording Shaw's death as in 1696, but the parish registers, school accounts book and Shaw's will all confirm that Calamy was incorrect.

41. L.R.O., Wills, 1695/1.

42. Joseph Alleine, *An Alarme to Unconverted Sinners....whereunto are annexed divers practical cases of conscience judiciously resolved* was first published in 1673.

43. *Report of the Charity Commissioners*, 32, part V, (Parliamentary Papers 1839, XV), pp. 345-6.

44. John Nichols, *History of Leicestershire* (1795-1815), Vol. 3 pt 2, p.617.

45. *Report of the Charity Commissioners*, 32, part V, (Parliamentary Papers 1839, XV), pp. 341-2.

46. L.R.O., Inventories, 1716.

47. J. & J.A. Venn, *Alumni Cantabrigienses*, Vol. I, p.69.

48. *Dictionary of National Biography.*

49. W. Lilly, *A History of His Life and Times* (1715), p.6.

50. H.L., Overseers of the Poor Accounts 1628-1634, Hastings Miscellaneous Box 12. A copy of this document is now at Ashby Museum.

51. L.M., ID 41/4/50, ff. 3-11.


CHAPTER 10: RELIGION

1. Quoted in W. Notestein, *The English People on the Eve of Colonization*, (1962), p.66.

2. A. Hildersham, *Lectures upon the Fourth of John* (1629), dedication.

3. Claire Cross, The Puritan Earl (1966), p.131.

4. A. Hildersham, *CLII Lectures upon Psalm LI* (1635), p. 708. *"Of this towne...I have knowne the tyme when it did shine as a light to all the countrey, and was famous among the Churches of Christ".*

5. C.W. Foster, *State of the Church*, Vol. I, Lincoln Records Society, Vol. 23, p.33.

6. L.M., ID/41/28/132.

7. Parish registers.

8. Prefixed to Knox, *Faithful Admonition* (1554).

9. P. Collinson, *Letters of Thomas Wood, Puritan, 1566-1577*, Bulletin of the Institute of Historical Research (1960 special supplement), p.24.

10. B.M., Addit. Mss. 29, f.546.

11. Cambr. Univ. Library, Mm 1.43 (Baker Mss 32), p.434.

12. *Dictionary of National Biography.*

13. L.R.O., ES AB/9/2.

14. B.M., Addit Mss. 27,632, f.49; the authorship is not known.

15. Ibid., f.49v.

16. Ibid., all quotations f. 47 and 47v.

17. L.M., ID 41/4/66.

18. L.M., ID 41/4/233.

19. C.D. Chalmers, *Puritanism in Leicestershire 1558-1633* (Leeds M.A. Thesis 1962), p.246.

20. Cambr. Univ. Library, Mm 1.43 (Baker Mss 32), p.426.

21. *Dictionary of National Biography.*

22. P. Collinson, The Elizabethan Puritan Movement (1967), p.452.

23. *Dictionary of National Biography.*

24. L.R.O., ES/AB/9/1, f. 28v.

25. *Report of the Charity Commissioners*, 32, part V, (Parliamentary Papers 1839, XV), pp. 347.

26. *Dictionary of National Biography.*

27. W. Lilly, *A History of His Life and Times* (1715), p.6.

28. C.D. Chalmers, *Puritanism in Leicestershire 1558-1633* (Leeds M.A. Thesis 1962), p.257.

29. L.M., ID 41/13/39, ff. 98-101.

30. L.M., ID 41/13/37, f. 64. The lists of those prosecuted in 1613 and 1614 do not survive.

31. L.M., ID 41/13/40, ff. 160-168.

32. L.M., ID 41/13/44, ff. 47-54.

33. L.M., ID 41/13/50, ff. 16-17, and L.M., ID 41/13/54, ff. 33-5.

34. L.M., ID 41/13/42, f.3.

35. L.M., ID 41/13/42, f.20.

36. L.M., ID 41/13/50, f.15v.

37. L.M., ID 41/13/50, f.146v.

38. L.R.O., ES/AB/9/1, f. 4v.

39. W. Scott, *The Story of Ashby-de-la-Zouch* (1907), p.384.

40. W. Lilly, *A History of His Life and Times* (1715), p.5.

41. H.L., HA Correspondence, 1028.

42. W. Scott, *The Story of Ashby-de-la-Zouch* (1907), p.385.

43. H.L., HA Correspondence, 7704.

44. L.M., ID 41/4/33, f. 109.

45. L.R.O., ES AB/9/1, f.52.

46. H.L., HA Correspondence, 10957 – presumably the *"grant of Liberty"* was the Act of Toleration of 1689.

47. P.R.O., E 179 240/279.

48. H.L., HA Correspondence, 7704.

49. A. Hildersham, *CLII Lectures upon Psalm LI* (1635), p. 708-710.

50. H.L., Book of Penal Laws, HAM Box 2.

51. L.M., ID 41/13/11, f. 91v; 41/13/37, f. 63v and 41/13/54, f. 73.

52. L.M. ID 41/13/37, f. 63v.

53. H.L., HA Miscellaneous, Box 12, 1. Churchwardens Accounts 1626-1636. A copy of this document is now in Ashby Museum.

54. L.M., ID 41/4/14, f.81.

55. L.M., ID 41/13/39, f.35.

56. L.M., ID 41/13/59, f.350v.

57. L.M., ID 41/13/58, f.350.

58. L.M., ID 41/13/59, f.349.

59. C.D. Chalmers, *Puritanism in Leicestershire 1558-1633* (Leeds M.A. Thesis 1962), p.259.

60. L.M., ID 41/13/58, ff. 10 & 21v.

61. L.M., ID 41/4/28, f.133 and 41/13/78, f. 121.

62. L.M., ID 41/13/64, ff. 139v & 143v.

63. L.M., ID 41/13/51, separate sheet between ff. 3v and 4.

64. C.D. Chalmers, *Puritanism in Leicestershire 1558-1633(1962)*, p.259.

65. Lincoln Archives, Miscellaneous Correspondence, Cor/M/2, f.38.

66. L.M., ID 41/13/57, f. 200.

67. L.M., ID 41/13/64, f. 126v.

68. L.M., ID 41/13/57, f 120v.

69. L.M., ID 41/13/64, f. 114.

70. L.M. stray paper 5D 33/463 in ID 41/13/58.

71. L.M. Glebe Terriers, 1674/5.

72. L.M., ID 41/4/273c.

73. L.M., ID 41/13/40, f. 20v.

74. L.M., ID 41/4/18, f 101.

75. H.L., [Leicestershire Manorial Box 29]; 41 of the 97 signatories made marks.

76. H.L., HA Correspondence, 7952.

77. H.L., HA Correspondence, 10956.

78. H.L., HA Correspondence, 10957.

79. H.L., HA Correspondence, 10958.

80. B.M., Mss Carte 78, f.186.


CHAPTER 11: THE MANORIAL LORD & THE TOWN COMMUNITY

1. H.L., [Leicestershire Manorial Box 1].

2. H.L., HA Correspondence, 7752. Mr Smart was the vicar.

3. Nicholas Carlisle, *A Concise Description of the Endowed Grammar Schools in England & Wales* (1818), Vol. I, pp. 742-751.

4. W. Scott *The Story of Ashby-de-la-Zouch (1907)*, p. 355.

5. H.L., *Book of Penal Laws*, HAM Box 2, p. 8a and 35. A copy of this document is now at Ashby Museum.

6. H.L., [LI K8, Box 61]. See above page 96.

7. H.L., HA Correspondence, 10951.

8. H.L., HA Correspondence, 2568.

9. H.L., [Leicestershire Manorial Box 28].

10. H.L., Hastings Accounts [Boxes 8 & 9].

11. H.L., Hastings Accounts [Boxes 8 & 14].

12. Claire Cross *The Puritan Earl* (1966), p.121.

13. H.L., [Leicestershire Local Affairs, Box 1].

14. Ibid., Of the two Ashby men sent abroad in 1624 one, John Weaver, was a shoemaker, aged 29; the other, Abraham Salt, a labourer, was aged 20. It seems that neither returned to Ashby.

15. H.L., HA Correspondence, 7794.

16. H.L., HA Correspondence, 10224 and 10246.

17. W. & J. Hextall, Ashby-de-la-Zouch (1852), p.50.

18. H.L., [LI W2, Box 21].

19. H.L., [Leicestershire Manorial Box 2].

20. H.L., [LI K8, Box 61].

21. H.L., [addendum to LI K8 Box 61], and HA Correspondence, 7672.

22. Nichols, *History of Leicestershire* (1804), Vol. III p. 617.

23. Quoted by W. Scott, *The Story of Ashby-de-la-Zouch* (1907), p.394.

24. L.M., ID 41/4/1170.

25. A. Hildersham, *Lectures upon the Fourth of John* (1629), Table of Contents, describing Lecture 67.

26. L.M., ID 41/13/64, p. 126a.

27. H.L., HA Miscellaneous, Box 12, 1. Churchwardens Accounts 1626-1636.

28. H.L., HA Miscellaneous, Box 12, 2.. Overseers of the Poor A/cs 1628-1634.

29. Joan Thirsk, *Agrarian History of England 1540-1640* (1967), p.255.

30. H.L., [Leicestershire Manorial Box 29].

31. H.L., HA Correspondence, 7761.

32. H.L., HA Correspondence, 10216.

33. L.M., ID 41/13/60, p. 145.

34. L.M., ID 41/4/273c.

35. L.M., ID 41/18/9, p. 4.

36. Calamy, The Ministers, *Lecturers, Masters and Fellows of Colleges and Schoolmasters, who were ejected or silenced after the Restoration in 1660* (2nd edition 1713) Vol II p. 429.

37. H.L., [LI K9, Box 62].

38. L.R.O., QS 6/1/2, p.159.

39. W. Scott, *The Story of Ashby-de-la-Zouch* (1907), p.272.

40. L.R.O., Wills, 1718.

# Index of names
(Note: the spelling of some names has been regularised)

Abny, family, *152*

Adcock ,William, *39*

Ainsworth, George, *100*

Alcocke, Mary, *116-7*

Alleine, Joseph, *113-4, 162*

Alleyne, John, *96, 141*

Anderson, Sir Edmund, *123*

Armeston, William, *117*

Armston, John, *40, 127*

Ash/e, family, *32*

Ashe, Abraham, *37, 142, 145*

Ashe, Francis, *59, 100*

Ashe, John (early 17C), *126*

Ash, John (late 17C), *32*

Ashe, Simeon, *59, 125*

Ash, Thomas, *32*

Ashe, William, *37*

Ashpinshaw, Thomas, *132*

Atkins, Joan, *77*

Atkins, William, *99*

Astley, William, *83, 90*

Ault, Professor, *10*

Aylmer, John, *120-1*

Bailey, John, *44*

Bainbrigg, John, *116*

Bainbrigg, Robert, *67, 116*

Bainbrigg, Thomas, *67, 99*

Bainbrigg, William, *78*

Barker, John, *26*

Barnes, Edward, *67*

Barnes, Margaret, *67*

Barry, Jonathan, *155*

Bateson, Mary, *156*

Baxter, Richard, *114*

Beadley, William, *144*

Beardsley, "young", *54, 116*

Beaumont, family, *16*

Beaumont, Henry de, *23*

Bell, Mr, *128*

Bennett, Martyn, *155-6*

Bentham, Thomas, *121*

Bentley, John, *127*

Bodell, James, *117*

Boulton, ?, *116*

Bowler, John, *142, 145, 147*

Bowman, Nicholas, *75*

Braddock, Margaret, *92*

Braddock, Mary, *92*

Bradshaw, William, *100*

Bramley, Roger, *64*

Bridgman, Lord Keeper, *108*

Brinsley, ?, *129*

Brinsley, John, *33, 100-1, 103-4, 106-7, 112, 126, 134, 149-50, 161*

Brookes, Job, *142*

Brookes, William, *116*

Broughton, Mr, *99*

Bryan, Nathaniel, *40*

Bucke, Isabell, *71*

Buckerfield, Widow, *55*

Burnell, Hugh, *23*

Burrowes, John, *33, 127, 129*

Burrowes, Margery, *127*

Burrowes, Thomas, *71*

Butler, James, Earl of Ormond, *24*

Buxston, Mr, *128, 135*

Byard, family, *37*

Byard, John, *77*

Byard, Peter, *58, 92*

Calamy, Edmund, *109-10, 162-5, 188, 192*

Calvin, John, *120*

Canner, Joseph, *44*

Cantrill, Robert, *89*

Carlisle, Nicholas, *140, 164*

Casey, family, *37*

Casey, Abraham, *39-40, 55*

Casey, Thomas, *67, 76*

Chalmers, C.D., *126, 131, 1337, 163-4*

Charles I, King, *39, 57*

Cheatle, Elizabeth, *117*

Cheatle, Richard, *43, 71*

Child, Laurence, *131*

Chiswell, William, *71*

Chomeley, Hugh, *100, 105, 161*

Clark, Peter, *154, 157*

Clarke, Henry, *116*

Clarke, S, *161*

Clarson, ?, *56*

Clarson, Timothy, *151-2*

Collier, James, *75*

Collinson, Patrick, *120, 162-3*

Compton, Bishop, *30, 128, 155*

Cooke, Richard, *91*

Cooper, Bishop, *121*

Copley, Hugh, *96*

Cotterell, Anne, *127*

Cotterell, Richard, *127*

Coverdale, Miles, *120*

Cox, John, *53*

Cox, Mr, *21*

Creswell, Mary, *95*

Cromwell, Oliver, *125*

Cross, Dr Claire, *118, 143, 155, 158, 161-2, 165*

Cundie, Thomas, *143*

Curtis, J, *158*

Curzon, Henry, *59*

Davenport, Thomas, *42*

Davis, Ferdinand, *71*

Davys, John, *69*

Dawson, Isaac, *115, 145*

Dawson, John, *115*

Doughty, Samuel, *128-9*

Doughty, Thomas, *128*

Downes, George, *99*

Draper, John (early 17C), *56, 130, 135*

Draper, John (late 17C), *132*

Eaglesfield, ?, *43, 71*

Eden, Sir Frederick Morton, *46, 156*

Edward IV, King, *24*

Elizabeth I, Queen, *123*

Elton, John, *37, 48-9, 83-4, 87, 142, 151*

Everitt, Professor Alan, *9-12, 85, 156*

Falkingham, John, *92*

Farmer, Lawrence, *117*

Farnell, Martin, *93-4, 96*

Farnham, G, *154-5, 158*

Ferryman, Robert, *87*

Field, John, *121*

Finberg, Professor H P R , *11, 154*

Firebrasse, "young", *56*

Fisscher, John, *23*

Fleming, William, *117*

Fosbrooke, T H, *156*

Foster, C W, *162*

Fowler, Nicholas, *94*

Fox, Dr Levi, *110, 155, 161-2*

French, Henry, *68*

Fuller, Thomas, *158*

Fullerton, Robert, *99*

Fyldes, Thurstan, *67*

Gilby, Anthony, *12, 52, 75, 99, 105, 120-2, 128 125, 150*

Gilby, Ester, *121*

Gilby, Nathaniel, *105*

Gininges, John, *82*

Godsbey, Richard, *53*

Goodman, Mary, *55*

Goodrich, Isabell, *132*

Goos, Robert, *23*

Goose, Nigel, *155*

Green, G H & M H, *154, 156*

Greene, John, *71*

Grey, Lord Thomas, *41*

Grindal, Archbishop, *121*

Hacket, William, *125-7*

Hakon, the "sutor", *23*

Hall, Hugh, *158*

Hall, Joseph, *100, 105, 161*

Hanley, Mr, *127*

Harding, Elizabeth, *55, 116*

Harris, Edward, *113*

Hassard, ?, *90*

Hassard, Edward, *77*

Hassard, John, *37*

Hassard, Robert, *131*

Hassard, Thomas, *37*

Hassard, William (late 16C), *75*

Hassard, William (mid 17C), *144*

Hastings, family, Earls of Huntingdon, *10-11, 16-7, 21, 24-28, 38-41, 43, 49-50, 56, 62-3, 71-2, 82, Chapter 11*

Hastings, Edward, Lord Loughborough, *41, 43*

Hastings, Ferdinando, 6th Earl of Huntingdon, *41, 43, 71*

Hastings, George, 4th Earl of Huntingdon, *125*

Hastings, Henry, 3rd Earl of Huntingdon, *39, 57, 64, 118- 9, 121-3, 125-6, 128, 138-140, 143*

Hastings, Henry, 5th Earl of Huntingdon, *57, 77, 81, 89, 125*

Hastings, Lucy, Countess of Huntingdon, *93, 128, 135, 137*

Hastings, Selina, Countess of Huntingdon, *145*

Hastings, Theophilus, 7th Earl of Huntingdon, *96, 129, 135, 137-40, 144*

Hastings, William, Lord, *24-6, 31, 63*

Hatterley, Joseph, *135, 147*

Hatterley, William, *75*

Heape, John, *131*

Henry VI, King, *24, 62*

Herrick, Robert, *38*

Hextall, W & J, *97, 155, 159, 161, 165*

Heywood, Thomas, *131*

Hildersham, Arthur, *33, 52 56, 79, 105, 122-8, 130, 134, 139, 147, 149-50, 162, 164-5*

Hildersham, Nathaniel, *56*

Hildersham, Samuel, *105*

Hill, Isabell, *56*

Hillier, Ken, 12

Hinckley, Richard, *59*

Holland, John (early 17C), *143*

Holland, John (late 17C), *58*

Hollins, Humphrey, *79, 94*

Hollinshed, Ottwell, *99*

Hood, William, *92, 128-9*
Hoskins, Professor W G, *10, 30, 53, 62-3, 76-7, 154-9*

Howe, John, *23*

Huntington, Henry E, *11*

Huntwicke, Richard, *53*

Jackson, Abraham, *54*

Jackson, Edward, *66*

Jackson, Rose, *147*

James I, King, *39, 57, 123*
Jaques, Mr, *47-9, 69, 72, 87, 140, 144, 149*

Jeffries, Lord Chancellor, *140*
Jones, Alexander, *135-7, 139, 149-50*

Jones, Chris, *61*

Jones, John, *161*

Jones, Robert, *12*

Jonson, Ben, *118*

Joyce, Isabell, *131*

Joyce, William, *66, 131*

Ketle, Hugh, *76*

King, David, *48, 92, 132*

Kirke, Humphrey, *31, 37, 155*

Kirkland, family, *151*

Knight, Mr, *137*

Knight, John, *55*

Knox, John, *162*

Laithwaite, J M W, *154*

Langley, William, *113-5, 145*

La Souche, family, *21, 24*

La Souche, Alan, *23*

La Souche, Roger, *22*

La Souche, William, *23, 65*

Laud, Archbishop, *100*

Leake, Francis, *92*

Lewin, James, *91*
Lilly, William, *65, 100-2, 104-5, 116, 128, 158, 161-3*

Loggan, John, *99*

Lord, John, *137-9*

Lord, Philip, *12*

Lyle, John, *25*

Lynes, Mr, *141*

Lyon, John, *133*

Mackay, John, *13, 154*

Manchester, Earl of, *125*

Mary I, Queen, *120*

Mason, Edward, *48, 94*

Meacock, Ralph, *36*

Moira, Lord, *146*

Monk, *65*

Moore, ?, *54*

Moore, Thomas, *44*

More, Sir John, *110*

Morley, William, *67*

Moseley, James, *151*

Narborowe, Ralph, *56, 132-3*

Nash, Thomas, *44*

Neile, Bishop Richard, *126*

Newton, Elizabeth, *127*

Newton, Alderman, *145*

Newton, Robert, *84*
Nichols, John, *21, 115, 154, 156, 158, 162, 165*

Nikolson, Hugh, *130*
Norden, John, *64*
Notestein, W, *162*
Ogilby, John, *155*
Orme, James, *58-9*
Orme, Robert, *104*
Orton, John, *86*
Pack, Christopher, *110*
Parker, Archbishop, *121*
Peach, Lara, *27*
Pemberton, Ambrose, *42*
Perrins, Simon, *55, 132, 148*
Perrins, Thomas, *55, 116, 148*
Pestell, Thomas, *126, 133-4*
Piddocke , family, *152*
Piddocke, Mr, *48-9, 69-70, 140, 144, 149*
Piddocke, John, *115*
Piddocke, Leonard, *115*
Pight, William, *131*
Pitt , William, *16, 154, 158*
Plucknett, Professor T F T, *82, 160*
Pole, Cardinal, *122*
Pratt, Thomas, *92*
Presbury, Henry (late 16C), *122*
Presbury, Henry (17/18C), *113*
Purchener, Margaret, *92*
Raylet, Robert, *117*
Richardson, Mary, *56*
Roby, John, *92*
Rogers, A, 157
Rogers, William, *1314*
Salmon, Vivian, *155*
Salt, Abraham, *165*
Sansom, Ann, *56, 147*

Savage, John, *113*
Save, Mr, *141*
Scott, W, *78-9, 141, 155, 159-60, 163-5*
Shaw, Sir John, *110*
Shaw, Samuel, *33, 109-113, 128, 145, 150, 162*
Shaw, Thomas, *109*
Sherwood, ?, *39*
Slack, Paul, *154, 157*
Smart, Ithiel (senior), *135, 142*
Smart, Ithiel (junior), *129, 137-40*
Smith, George, *145*
Smith, Job, *96, 141*
Smith, Richard (died 1616), *68*
Smith, Richard (living in 1634), *131*
Smith, Samuel, *37*
Smythe, William, *52, 67, 99*
Soresby, Thomas, *71*
Spencer, Richard, *79, 134, 149-50*
Stocks, Helen, *156*
Swaine, John, *49, 69*
Swindell, George, *35, 140*
Sykes, Francis, *51*
Sykes, Henry (1640s), *42*
Sykes, Henry (17/18C), *59*
Sykes, Nicholas (early 17C), *131*
Sykes, Nicholas (late 17C), *93*
Symonds, Richard, *41-29, 156*
Taylor, Edward, *92*
Taylor, John, *44*
Taylor, Thomas, *131*
Taylyer, William, *76*
Thirsk, Dr Joan, *9-10, 12, 148, 156-7, 165*
Thompson, A Hamilton, *155*

Throne, Anthony, *92*

Tomlinson, John, *77*

Tomlinson, William, *56*

Trenthom, Leonard, *35, 68*

Turner, ?, *145*

Venn, J & J A, *162*

Vinson, Richard, *35*

Wake, Bishop, *30*

Wakelyn, Clement, *135*

Wakelyn, William, *135*

Walker, William, *44*

Ward, George, *103*

Watson, Abraham, *54*
Watson, Anthony, *35, 134-5, 147, 150*

Watson, John, *104*

Weaver, John, *165*

White, A, *161-2*

Whitefield, George, *145*

Whiteman, Anne, *155*
Widdowes, Thomas, *99, 120-3, 128*

Wigston, William, *52*

Wilkins, Elizabeth, *59*

Wodhous, Robert, *25*

Wood, Daniel, *83-4, 92*

Wood, Humphrey, *132*

Wood, Thomas, *121, 162*

Woodcocke, Edward, *40*

Wright, Margery, *59, 61, 90, 158*

Wycliffe, John, *118*